05/0012

Waterside, Po...

This book

Hindquarters: Loin very sturdy, broad and gently arched, quarters well covered round and muscular, the second thigh is long and well developed, the stifle well turned, and the hocks set low. From the rear the hocks should be quite straight, with the feet turning neither in nor out.

Tail: Customarily completely docked.

Coat: Profuse, of good harsh texture, not straight, but shaggy and free from curl. Undercoat of waterproof pile. Head and skull well covered with hair, ears moderately coated, neck well coated, forelegs well coated all round, hindquarters more heavily coated than rest of body. Quality, texture, and profusion to be considered above mere length.

Colour: Any shade of grey, grizzle or blue. Body and hindquarters of solid colour with or without white socks. White patches in the solid area to be discouraged. Head, neck, forequarters and under belly to be white with or without markings. Any shade of brown undesirable.

Feet: Small, round and tight, toes well arched, pads thick and hard. Dew claws should be removed.

Size: Height: dogs: 61 cms (24 ins) and upwards; bitches: 56 cms (22 ins) and upwards. Type and symmetry of greatest importance, and on no account to be sacrificed to size alone.

P. T. O.

St Helens
College
Library

Old English Sheepdog

◇

by Ann Arch

Table of Contents

9

History of the Old English Sheepdog

From 'Shepherd's Dog' to 'Sheepdog' to the dog we know today as the Old English Sheepdog or Bobtail, this breed has grown from the obscure beginnings of herding dogs into one of the world's most familiar breeds. Follow the breed's evolution and learn about the important people and dogs in OES history.

20

Characteristics of the Old English Sheepdog

Best known for his abundant fluffy coat, the Old English Sheepdog has a lot of personality under all that hair! Learn about the breed's playful demeanour, unique physical characteristics and health considerations, and find out if you're the right owner for a Bobtail.

26

Breed Standard for the Old English Sheepdog

Learn the requirements of a well-bred Old English Sheepdog by studying the description of the breed set forth in The Kennel Club standard. Both show dogs and pets must possess key characteristics as outlined in the breed standard.

34

Your Puppy Old English Sheepdog

Be advised about choosing a reputable breeder and selecting a healthy, typical puppy. Understand the responsibilities of ownership, including home preparation, acclimatisation, the vet and prevention of common puppy problems.

60

Everyday Care of Your Old English Sheepdog

Enter into a sensible discussion of dietary and feeding considerations, exercise, grooming, travelling and identification of your dog. This chapter discusses Old English Sheepdog care for all stages of development.

PUBLISHED IN THE
UNITED KINGDOM BY:

INTERPET
PUBLISHING

Vincent Lane, Dorking
Surrey RH4 3YX
England

ISBN 1-902389-37-9

84
Housebreaking and Training Your Old English Sheepdog

by Charlotte Schwartz
Be informed about the importance of training your Old English Sheepdog from the basics of housebreaking and understanding the development of a young dog to executing obedience commands (sit, stay, down, etc.).

PHOTO CREDITS

Norvia Behling
Carolina Biological Supply
Doskocil
Isabelle Francais
James Hayden-Yoav
James R Hayden, RBP
Carol Ann Johnson
Dwight R Kuhn

Dr Dennis Kunkel
Mikki Pet Products
Phototake
Jean Claude Revy
Alice Roche
Dr Andrew Spielman
C James Webb

Illustrations by Renée Low
The publisher wishes to thank Maryanne Henry, William & Jan Lichtenberger, John Perry, Arlene Pietrocola and the rest of the owners of dogs featured in this book.

144
Your Senior Old English Sheepdog

Recognise the signs of an ageing dog, both behavioural and medical; implement a senior-care programme with your veterinary surgeon and become comfortable with making the final decisions and arrangements for your senior Old English Sheepdog.

113
Health Care of Your Old English Sheepdog

Discover how to select a proper veterinary surgeon and care for your dog at all stages of life. Topics include vaccination scheduling, skin problems, dealing with external and internal parasites and the medical and behavioural conditions common to the breed.

148
Showing Your Old English Sheepdog

Experience the dog show world, including different types of shows and the making up of a champion. Go beyond the conformation ring to working trials and agility trials, etc.

Index: 156

Copyright © 2000 Animalia, Ltd.
Cover patent pending. Printed in Korea.

Old English Sheepdog

An English farmer, circa 1892, with a pair of working Old English Sheepdogs. The OES was at one time the most popular working breed.

Old English Sheepdogs are active, dedicated and hard-working yet fun-loving dogs. Their instinctive herding traits and abilities are evident in the breed even as pups.

The background of the breed is certainly 'misty.' In Brian Vesey-Fitzgerald's 1948 *The Book of the Dog*, the author recounts the earliest reference to the Old English Sheepdog breed made by Columella. Famous artists such as Van Eyck and Dürer painted portraits of dogs resembling the Bobtail as early as the 15th century.

In the early 1700s, George-Louis Leclerc, known as Count de Buffon, describes 37 different varieties of dogs, including the Shepherd's Dog in the first group. The Shepherd's Dogs were described as having sharp fox-like muzzles, erect ears and an instinct for protecting flocks. All of these features still apply to various shepherding breeds today. The breeding of types suited to different terrains and climatic conditions undoubtedly brought about the breeds that we now know. In *The Sportsman's Cabinet,* there is a recognisable early Bobtail by the artist Reinagle.

Though early writings refer to Shepherd's Dogs, the name gradually changed to Sheepdogs. In 1884, the Collie is described as being either Scottish or Welsh, although many historians believe that the original, true Shepherd's Dog was English. In 1872, Stonehenge wrote of the English Sheepdog as being '. . . rough or smooth, in various colours. . .

9

account from 1883 worth noting was written by Idstone. He describes the sheepdogs in the southern counties of England, including Oxfordshire, Wiltshire, Berkshire, Hampshire, and Dorset. He regarded them as 'typical English Sheepdogs—blue, grizzled, rough-haired, large-limbed, surly, small-eared, small-eyed, leggy, bob-tailed dogs.' He also noted that the rare specimen would run over the backs of the flock, to lead them into a lane.

In the *Kennel Encyclopaedia* (1910), editor Sidney Turner purports a possible connection of the sheepdog to the Russian Ovcharka. In later publications, authors tell accounts of the Smithfield Collie, being used as a droving dog, taking the flocks of sheep and herds of cattle from the southern counties of England to

Top: The Komondor, a Hungarian flock- and herd-guarding breed with a distinctive corded coat, is reputed to have a hand in the genetic history of the OES. Bottom: The Bearded Collie certainly looks like a relative of the OES.

[including] grizzle, black, red, brindled or (for the most part) white . . . [and] a dull rust colour, patched with black… [The smooth] variety has frequently what are called "china" or "walled" eyes . . .' Of historical interest also was Stonehenge's commentary about the docking of sheepdogs: 'The Shepherd's dog, under old excise laws, was only exempt from tax when the tail was cut off, so it was formerly removed.'

Various other accounts of the breed's origins exist. One famous

DID YOU KNOW?

Since dogs have been inbred for centuries, their physical and mental characteristics are constantly being changed to suit man's desires for hunting, retrieving, scenting, guarding and warming their master's laps. During the past 150 years, dogs have been judged according to physical characteristics as well as functional abilities. Few breeds can boast a genuine balance between physique, working ability and temperament.

the famous Smithfield Meat Market in London.

The Old English Sheepdog has been featured in various book illustrations and pictures over the years. Apart from the famed Reinagle, there is a well-known oil painting by Gainsborough of the Duke of Buccleuch in 1771 with a recognisable dog. In 1835, Sidney Cooper painted a fine example of an Old English Sheepdog of blue and white colouring, with good head and bone.

The breed eventually became stabilised and numerically strong enough in some areas to merit attention from dog show organisers. At a show in Birmingham (later to become the home of world-famous Crufts Dog Show, at the National Exhibition Centre) held in 1873, there were three exhibitors, but the judge found the quality so poor that he withheld the first prize—only awarding a second placing! This could have deterred fanciers for a while, until interest was aroused by Mr Freeman-Lloyd. In 1889 an informative leaflet was produced by Mr Freeman-Lloyd, which promoted the newly formed Old English Sheepdog Club, serving to attract quite a few newcomers to the breed. Fortunately, the breed continued to appear at the shows.

Many journalists and writers from this early period were outspoken about the breed, its

The South Russian Ovcharka, top, and the Middle-Asian Ovcharka, shown below, have been mentioned in the ancestry of the OES, but no firm proof of such a relationship has ever been discovered.

qualities and shortcomings. These uninhibited writers surely helped shepherd the breed towards greater stability and uniformity, and could be relied upon to focus attention on the breed's progress. Although many of these early authors have not been credited with all they did for the breed, one outspoken, well-spoken lady who will never be forgotten is Mrs Fare Fosse, who was the first female president of the OES Club, and the owner of the famous bitch Champion Fairweather. This bitch can still be seen, for upon her death, her body went to a taxidermist, and

Mr Dickson's Harkaway and Ch Lady Scaramouche. Dr Dickson owned Ch Handsome Boy, bred in 1902, who was later sold to an American owner. Other well-reported dogs at the turn of the century were Mr Weager's Ch. Dairymaid, Mr Clayton's Ch Victor Cavendish and Mr Wilmot's Ch Robert the Bobby and Sergeant Bruce. The previously mentioned bitch Ch Fairweather was very successful in the show ring, having won no less than 20 Challenge Certificates in her career. She had a famous predecessor in the kennel called Wall-Eyed Bob, who was another prolific winner.

Undoubtedly the most famous kennels in the world were at Shepton Mallet in Somerset, the home of the Tilley family. 'W T S' founded them, his brother 'H A' took over upon his death, with his daughter Florence, continuing them upon his death until her own death.

So many of us went to Shepton for our first Old English Sheepdog, and my first Bobtail was from one of the last litters bred with Shepton parentage on both sides, back in 1962. Some pedigrees can still trace back to Shepton even now. Shepton breeding went out all over the world including to the US. The OES Club of America was founded in 1904 by H A Tilley, who crossed the Atlantic many

she is now part of the special canine section in the Country Annexe of the Natural History Museum at Tring in Hertfordshire.

Other famous dogs that contributed to the future of the breed were Dr Locke's Ch Sir Cavendish (1887), winner at shows in 1890, '91 and '92; Dr Bott's Ch Bouncer; Dr MacGill's Ch Watch Boy; Sir Humphrey de Trafford's Ch Dame Barbara; and times in order to exhibit his stock. This was a lengthy undertaking in days prior to air travel.

In more recent times, many have put pen to paper, producing books on the breed, but perhaps the book that is still eagerly sought by true enthusiasts is that by Aubrey Hopwood (1905). H A Tilley also wrote a very collectible book in 1937. Rowland Johns edited *Our Friends, the Old English and Shetland Sheepdog* in 1935. In those earlier days, the tendency was for general dog books with chapters devoted to specific breeds. One that is still valued is Hutchinson's *Dog Encyclopaedia*, which devoted 26 pages to the Old English Sheepdog. Another general

DID YOU KNOW?

Dogs and wolves are members of the genus *Canis*. Wolves are known scientifically as *Canis lupus* while dogs are known as *Canis domesticus*. Dogs and wolves are known to interbreed. The term canine derives from the Latin derived word *Canis*. The term dog has no scientific basis but has been used for thousands of years. The origin of the word dog has never been authoritatively ascertained.

One of the more common of the Ovcharka breeds, the Caucasian Ovcharka.

publication that I have treasured through the years is Vero Shaw's *The Illustrated Book of the Dog* (1881).

Over the years, the Bobtail has been used for advertising for a variety of commercial products. Perhaps the most famous in the past thirty years is Dulux Paints, which originally featured the late Mr and Mrs Sharpe's Shepton Daphnis Horsa, otherwise known as Dash. He was replaced upon his retirement, as the result of a national competition, by Mr and

Bob and Dairy Maid, two famous sheepdogs of 1892. You can see the resemblance between these dogs and today's OES.

Mrs Norman Harrison's Ch Fernville Lord Digby. Due to great demand for the 'Dulux Dog' to make appearances at charity affairs and other events, various owners and dogs were recruited in order to keep up with the demand! Many people were attracted to the breed, and as a result, breeding and registrations increased considerably. This in turn put pressure on to the OES Rescue, which was taking in dogs that had been purchased in haste without sufficient knowledge of what was required from an owner. At one time, the number of dogs being abandoned and rescued exceeded 100 per month! Thankfully, the breed had now

Colin and his happy handler at the prestigious Manchester show of 1880. Colin won Second Prize and was chosen Reserve Champion; a Manchester win was considered a very high honour.

14

settled down to many fewer litters bred, for a more informed ownership.

Films have also accounted for promotion of the Bobtail, with one called Lord Nelson perhaps the best known for his appearances in the US. *The Shaggy Dog, Summer Magic* and *Chitty Chitty Bang Bang* were earlier and very successful productions. *Digby—The Biggest Dog* in the World used Mrs Pat Creed's Mosshall Lady Joy in the early and latter parts, while Mr and Mrs Glass's Twotrees Brandysnap took the part where the star grew gigantic through drinking a chemical.

WHY IS THE OES CALLED THE 'BOBTAIL'?

Many years ago, when a government needed to raise money, it applied taxes to various things. One was on the number of windows in a house—that is why you will see some old houses in Britain, with their window frames

bricked up. Another means of generating revenue was to put a tax on dogs, with the only exemption being a farmer's working animal. In order to prove that these dogs were indeed workers, the tax relief could only be claimed if they had their tails removed in order that they could be undoubtedly identified by the tax collector!

IS THE OES RELATED TO ANY OTHER IDENTIFIABLE BREEDS?

Although a relationship between the OES and the Russian Ovcharka has been referenced in a number of sources, no cynologist has proved this relationship

Early American champions were Downderry Voyager (left) and Irresistible (right), owned by Mrs Walter Roesler. They created quite a stir at the Westminster Kennel Club's 55th Annual Show held in New York City in 1927.

definitively. In fact, there are more than one breed known as Ovcharkas in Russia, including the Caucasian, Middle-Asian and South Russian. Practically all European countries had their own type of rough-coated farmers' dogs, and their coat type was

Mme J Plaim and Mrs Gordon with their OES at the 1933 Paris Dog Show. The breed was quite frequently seen in France.

Ch Tommy Tittlemouse was a noted champion and sire of many other champions during the 1920s.

Helen Cluff of New York City, preparing her Old English Sheepdog for the show; circa 1932. All that was needed was brushing and combing, along with combing up of the leg hair.

influenced by the weather conditions in which they worked. Some eventually emerged more as flock- and herd-guarding breeds (such as the Maremma Sheepdog of Italy and the giant corded

Ch Dame Barbara was one of the champions from Sir H de Trafford's famous kennel in the 1920s.

Komondor of Hungary, etc.), while others were working the animals and escorting (droving) them to markets. Some experts suggest that there is a link to the Polish Lowland Sheepdog, which some people believe is merely a small

Int. Ch Dolly Grey, bred by Mr F H Travis, was a winning champion in both the UK and the USA in the 1930s.

The Old English Sheepdog was, and still is, popular around the world. Here is an example of the breed in Germany during the 1920s.

normally removed at two to four days of age. In the past, well-experienced breeders did this very competently, but now the law in Britain only permits qualified veterinary surgeons to undertake this. With the new legislation, the

edition of the Bobtail. These small Polish dogs were used in many ways, and it is well documented that they travelled to Scotland on the boats of traders from Central Europe, where they accompanied farm animals for sale. It is however more likely that the Polish Lowland Sheepdog is in the background of the Bearded Collie than the Bobtail. However, when looking at early pictures of Bearded Collies, even they could easily be linked to early Old English Sheepdogs!

CAN A BOBTAIL EVER BE BORN WITHOUT A TAIL?
Rarely, but it has been known to occur occasionally. Tails are

The Duke of Beucleugh, shown in this magnificent portrait by Gainsborough, is accompanied by what is claimed to be the first representation of an Old English Sheepdog in a painting. Some experts think that the dog is too small to be an OES.

Wall-Eyed Bob is one of the most famous in the breed's history. He was sold for 20 shillings at a public house and was later owned by Mr J Thomas and by Mrs Fare Fosse, one of the most prominent people in the breed.

removal of tails is now illegal in the Scandinavian and some other European countries; in some other countries, after a designated date, docked dogs will no longer be allowed to compete in shows.

DOES HAVING A TAIL AFFECT THE ACTION OF THE BREED?
I find that it has affected the characteristic movement on some that I have judged. The natural tendency when moving is for the tail to be lifted. In some dogs, this appears to take away some of the stronger hind action. The mechanics of movement are the same, but the actual steps appear lighter and lack that strong driving action.

DID YOU KNOW THAT PAUL MCCARTNEY HAD A BOBTAIL?
Do you remember the song entitled 'Martha, My Dear'? Martha was purchased just prior to the Beatles tour of India, and she came back for house-training. Originally Paul called her Knickers, but a friend felt that it was inappropriate and so she was re-named Martha. She was the forerunner of several that he and his wife Linda owned in later years.

This old photo was captioned 'Three Beauties.' It shows the immensely popular film star Jean Harlow and her two Old English Sheepdogs. Miss Harlow was a great lover of dogs.

19

CHARACTERISTICS OF THE
OLD ENGLISH SHEEPDOG

Lively, friendly and people-oriented, the Old English Sheepdog is happiest when he's part of the action and spending time with his family.

The Bobtail is quite lively and loves to be a part of family life. If he is allowed to repay you for your time and attention, then nothing makes him happier.

From the breed's early origins as the shepherd's droving dog, the Bobtail retains these natural instincts. The dormant need to herd and drove remains. Dogs have been known to become quite concerned when the children of family are scattered around the garden, and will earnestly try quite hard to herd them up together. Having been used for accompanying flocks and herds to market, sometimes over several days, there is still the need to take quite a fair amount of exercise. So don't ever imagine that you can make the breed into a 'couch potato.' Because it was used for travelling great distances, the Bobtail often moves with a pacing action, when the legs on each side move in parallel with each other. Pacing is used as a resting type of action, to conserve energy for later on. This type of action is commonly seen in some horses.

The Bobtail has a bright and lively personality. His reaction to the varied activities of a family is

to usually show a desire to become a part of it. This can range from walking with mother to take the children to school, to enjoying a whole day out, to walking in the country. The Bobtail loves to play, especially with anyone who has the energy. Football is always a favourite. On a serious note—the choice of ball should be carefully considered. A ball that is small can easily be swallowed or become stuck in the throat with dire results. We always found that the rather large, tough plastic footballs gave the greatest fun, but sometimes their life duration was not so very long. A strong jaw on a ball can lead very quickly to a puncture. They love to 'go fetch'—again the choice of toy that can be thrown for their retrieval should be carefully made. Something that is too soft and chewy can quickly break up and be ingested. There is now a great variety of specially formed, toughened toys, which come in large enough sizes not to be chewed and swallowed.

With their underlying ability to work, the Bobtail can be trained. Patience and humour are necessary, but the breed has been known to perform in basic and even advanced obedience and agility. Some breeds have not started to take part in tests of herding ability, but it should be remembered that the Bobtail was not used to move sheep the way a Border Collie does and therefore cannot be expected to instinctively perform in this manner, cutting and driving the flock. The Bobtail not only displays

DOGS, DOGS, GOOD FOR YOUR HEART

People usually purchase dogs for companionship, but studies show that dogs can help to improve their owners' health and level of activity, as well as lower a human's risk of coronary heart disease. Without even realising it, when a person puts time into exercising, grooming and feeding a dog, he also puts more time into his own personal health care. Dog owners

establish a more routine schedule for their dogs to follow, which can have positive effects on a human's health. Dogs also teach us patience, offer unconditional love and provide the joy of having a furry friend to pet!

OES are very strong chewers and only durable toys made especially for dogs should be offered to them.

trainability but it can also show great patience. Our first Bobtail would happily allow my son to dress him up, with scarves and hats, and when my daughter started to walk, the dog was her best helper. She would crawl

This Australian Terrier isn't intimidated by his new big fluffy friend. Bobtails do well in multiple-pet households provided that the dogs are introduced and allowed to get to know each other.

Routine coat care is essential to keep the Bobtail's profuse coat healthy and tangle-free. This is a necessary aspect of the dog's care to which the owner must commit.

across to him, and slowly pull herself up one of his legs, and then they would slowly walk along together. Even as a puppy, he displayed the greatest patience and tolerance. He would also happily allow himself to be a pillow—for a child laying on the floor or sofa.

Our dogs were treated almost as other children, and that is the way I like to think of any family dog—as an extension to the family unit. Whenever I was considering whether a family was suitable to adopt one of our Bobtail puppies, I would use their children to evaluate them. If the children were acceptably behaved, then I believe that the parents could cope with a Bobtail.

As with all families, routine and kind but firm discipline is

essential if they and the dog are to be acceptable members of the community. Over-indulgence and lack of control can soon lead to poor behaviour. The new, cute, fluffy puppy may be attractive to all, but that is no excuse for over-indulging him. With intelligent dogs, even at a few weeks of age, they will soon try to get their own way, so gentle but firm control must never be ignored.

Establishment of a daily routine is soon accomplished, and this involves regular times to be put out to avoid little puddles indoors, feeding, exercise, etc. When you first take your puppy home, it's hard to resist the temptation to go out for long walks. Remember, the pup is still very young and can tire easily. When all inoculations are complete, and it is safe for the

puppy to go out, short walks are ample. Food converts into the energy required for growth, so if too much energy is used up in exercise and play, then development may suffer.

As a family dog, the Bobtail is unsuitable for shutting out in kennels all of the time. They react and develop much better, if they are able to be a part of everyday activities. There will be times when they cannot be a part of everything, but to exclude them totally can lead to a miserable and frustrated dog.

Care of coat is essential. The puppy will have a shortish and rather soft coat to start with, which will soon start to grow longer and thicker. Regularity is necessary, and this also applies to grooming. Also, care of diet is another thing that should be taken quite seriously. The working Bobtail has never needed or been indulged in exotic or high-protein foods. Our own experience was that a plain and unvaried diet of low protein is most suitable. To keep varying can soon lead to a confused digestive system, resulting in stomach upsets. With a growing and quite profuse coat, the last thing that an owner wants to experience is an upset tummy. In earlier days, we sampled a rather small quantity of new food, and I can't tell you what an awful experience it was to have six Bobtails, all in full mature coats,

OES are large dogs and they must be educated and disciplined at an early age or getting them into a bath or onto a grooming table would be a nightmare.

and all with upset and loose digestions.

ARE YOU A BOBTAIL PERSON?

Firstly, the owner must be prepared to make a full commitment to caring. Dogs are not soft toys to be purchased on impulse, picked up, and then discarded. They are living, feeling and caring beings, so if you honestly cannot accept what their needs are, then dog ownership should be avoided. As with all breeds, prospective owners can be captivated by an appealing picture. That is merely the icing on the cake. To maintain the dog in acceptable condition entails regularity in all connected duties—training and associated discipline, feeding, exercising and nutrition. As the Bobtail coat grows, not only will it look quite beautiful in maturity, but there will come the inevitable seasonal discarding of jacket. If you have a picture-book home, and a few dogs hairs floating around the floor or sticking to upholstery will offend you, then the choice of breed should be very carefully considered. We may all have rooms forbidden to family pets, but if pets are to be unacceptable anywhere indoors, then your reasons for having the breed should be re-evaluated. For those who love the breed, and are able to deal with the necessary feeding and exercising, but cannot cope with regular grooming, then consider a pet clip. There are many happy dogs, living a normal life, whose coats are kept in this convenient trimmed state. My own gradual withdrawal from ownership was because arthritic pain had started after hours of brushing and combing, getting coats into showing condition. Not wanting to face a future of clipped-off dogs that I would not be able to exhibit, I came to the sad conclusion that I was not longer fit enough to do justice to the breed, and felt that it would be cruel to them to risk matting-up.

THE BEST HOME FOR A BOBTAIL

There are Bobtails who live happily in cities; whereas other dogs have the availability of large gardens in suburbia; and others enjoy unlimited access to country-side. Your ability to deal with exercise requirements is very important. I have known dogs who lived in flats, but were well cared for, with regular exercise and attention. There have also been owners who restricted access to the garden for fear of urine spoiling plants and lawns. Understanding garden lovers will make sure that they allocate a doggy area for their pets. Providing that puppies are trained early enough as to where they may relieve themselves, then everyone can be happy. Just as much as their toilet activity needs to be directed early on, control-ling and discouraging digging around growing trees, bushes, and lawns are essential. The baby puppy should be corrected whenever such misdeeds are attempted.

Due to its heavy coat, the Old English Sheepdog will not normally wish to be kept very warm. However, our experience of the breed is that if they live in a house that is never very cold, then their undercoat will not grow quite so thick.

Opposite page: Are you capable of adjusting your life to accommodate an Old English Sheepdog? Owning a dog of any breed requires a full commitment, but a large, heavily coated breed like the OES requires extra time and dedication on the owner's part.

OLD ENGLISH SHEEPDOG

All purebred dogs have a breed standard. This is perhaps best equated to a 'blueprint'—the ideal that one aims for when breeding—the ideal that one seeks when judging—a fit, sound and typical animal that should still be suited to the task for which it was originally bred.

Modern show presentation has emphasised 'hair dressing' in appearance, and too often the correctly constructed, fit, healthy, well-muscled dog underneath has been sacrificed. However much we want our dogs to look good, we must never ignore the balanced and solid construction that the drover's dog needed.

The breed standard is divided up into easily understandable sections, which are placed in the

This show dog is Ch Baggybush Master of Madness at Dantrelar.

order that a judge in the show ring will follow. The author's interpretation and comments on the standard appear in italics.

THE KENNEL CLUB STANDARD FOR THE OLD ENGLISH SHEEPDOG

General Appearance: Strong, square-looking dog with great symmetry and overall soundness. Absolutely free from legginess, profusely coated all over. A thick-set, muscular, able-bodied dog with a most intelligent expression. The natural outline should not be artificially changed by scissoring or clipping.

You only have to look at the long, leaner head of a Deerhound, or the finely chiselled head on a Poodle, to see just how the Bobtail should NOT look! In current times, when great emphasis has been placed on coat for the show ring, it would be interesting to see some exhibits either with coats shaved off or dripping wet in a bath! The Bobtail is a breed that was called upon to work in all terrain, so it must have good body and strong limbs. The side view of the breed, if you imagine it without head and neck, should just about fit in to a square.

Characteristics: Of great stamina, exhibiting a gently rising topline, and a pear-shaped body when

viewed from above. The gait has a typical roll when ambling or walking. Bark has a distinctive toned quality.

A particular point of the breed was its bark, and as we don't expect a show dog to demonstrate this, reference to that has now been deleted.

Temperament: A biddable dog of even disposition, Bold, faithful and trustworthy, with no suggestion of nervousness or unprovoked aggression.

Head and Skull: In proportion to the size of the body. Skull capacious, rather square. Well arched above eyes, stop well defined. Muzzle strong, square and truncated, measuring approximately half of the total head length. Nose large and black. Nostrils wide.

The head is described as having a rather square and capacious skull, with arches over the eyes, and an identifiable 'stop'—which is the indentation between the eyes where the head

The OES gait is very different than most other breeds. The term 'bear-like roll' is used to describe the dog while walking, and the standard also mentions that the head is naturally carried low when the dog is in motion.

Correct head with proper fall.

The eyes are hard to see on a Bobtail in full coat, but this dog's haircut allows a clear view of 'wall-eye'—one dark and one light eye. This dog also has the desired dark rim pigmentation.

raises up from the level of the topline of the muzzle. There is a call for a strong jaw, which helps to give the head its powerful appearance. Weak jaws look snipey. The nose should be large and black. A hard-working dog needs a good-sized nose with large nostrils. If the nose were small and the nostrils pinched, there would be a lack of air flowing into the lungs and the bloodstream. This would bring about an easily tired dog, incapable of working for long hours. The outer appearance of the nose should be 'wet.'

Working out in strong sunshine, a dog with a nose lacking pigment would soon become burned and sore, whereas eye rims would not be so exposed to the sun, being shaded by head coat falling forward. On a puppy, one can sometimes find incomplete nose pigmentation, which is referred to as a 'butterfly nose.'

Eyes: Set well apart. Dark or wall eyes. Two blue eyes acceptable. Light eyes undesirable. Pigmentation on the eye rim is preferred.

The eyes should be dark or wall-eyes. A good dark eye shows depth and intelligence. Paler eyes appear to lack character and expression. 'Wall-eye' is the term to describe one dark eye and one blue eye. The blue eye should be of good colour and well defined, for a pearly-grey shade gives absolutely nothing to the expression. Also acceptable are two blue eyes. They are not then called 'double wall-eyes' but referred to as 'china' or 'blue.' Again, they should be of good colour and well defined. Good pigment around the eye rims is highly desirable, though in some bloodlines the achievement of fully pigmented rims can take

Correct head with topknot.

the jaws meet evenly, the teeth will touch each other, edge to edge, in what is called a level bite. In this instance, the teeth will wear down. In the past, a level bite was acceptable, but currently I would say that it is tolerated, but not really desired. The ideal bite is the 'scissor' where the upper teeth just

several years! Allowance is made for the gradual development of pigmented rims, but when it is lacking on the nose, there is not the same tolerance into maturity.

Ears: Small and carried flat to side of head.

The ears are ideally small and neat, but all too often they are larger than desirable. When heavily coated, then can prevent air reaching the inner parts of the ear, and if not carefully checked on a regular basis, problems soon develop.

Mouth: Teeth strong, large, and evenly placed. Scissor bite–jaws strong with a perfect, regular and complete scissor bite, i.e. upper teeth closely overlapping lower teeth and set square to the jaws. Pincer tolerated but undesirable.

Strong teeth, evenly placed around the jaws are needed. If

EXPENSE OF BREEDING

The decision to breed your dog is one that must be considered carefully and researched thoroughly before moving into action. Some people believe that breeding will make their bitch happier or that it is an easy way to make money. Unfortunately, indiscriminate breeding only worsens the

rampant problem of pet overpopulation, as well as putting a considerable dent in your pocketbook. As for the bitch, the entire process from mating through whelping is not an easy one and puts your pet under considerable stress. Last, but not least, consider whether or not you have the means to care for an entire litter of pups. Without a reputation in the field, your attempts to sell the pups may be unsuccessful.

Gait/Movement: When walking, exhibits a bear-like roll from the rear. When trotting, shows effort-less extension and strong driving rear action, with legs moving straight along line of travel. Very elastic at the gallop. At slow speeds, some dogs may tend to pace. When moving, the head carriage may adopt a naturally lower position.

Movement needs to be strong and easy. Good shoulder construction should give correct forward reach, and the sound rear with correctly low-set hock will provide strong propulsion. A problem that sometimes appears is that the hock joint lacks strength. Sometimes called 'popping' or sub-luxating hock, it will not resist pressure applied from behind, and slopes forward. When hocks are thus weakened, there is the inability to give good strong driving action. When an animal has two poor hock joints, the hind movement will appear to be quite even, whereas the combination of one weak and one strong joint will surely display uneven action to those observing it moving away. Such weakness can be seen fairly easily when watching profile action, as there is an unpleasing carriage, rather than that of the strong forward thrust. That is a very good reason for requiring dogs not to be moved too fast when judging them!

Coat: Profuse, of good harsh texture, not straight, but shaggy and free from curl. Undercoat of waterproof pile. Head and skull well covered with hair, ears moderately coated, neck well coated, forelegs well coated all round, hindquarters more heavily coated than rest of body. Quality, texture, and profusion to be consid-ered above mere length.

The coat should be profuse, of good crisp texture, but not curly. The undercoat should be soft and waterproof. Though curly coat is incorrect, the outer hair is not perfectly straight, but has what is called 'break' —a slight move away from being dead straight.

Colour: Any shade of grey, grizzle or blue. Body and hindquarters of solid colour with or without white socks. White patches in the solid area to be discouraged. Head, neck, forequarters and under belly to be white with or without markings. Any shade of brown undesirable.

Colour can be grey in all its shades, grizzle, blue or blue-merle. (We rarely see the patchy merle of old, which was originally called 'marled,' a derivative or slang version of 'marbled.') Coat with or without white markings. We very rarely see dogs without quite a notable amount of white in their coat markings, which is an indica-tion of fashion for the show ring. In the past, we saw excellent specimens with very little white

Breed gait: walk/pace.

Breed gait: fast trot.

markings, but fashion appears to have carried the day! Brown in the coat is highly undesirable—coat that dies and is not removed will go quite reddish brown. 'Mis-marks' are not encouraged, and puppies born with large white patches in the whole body coloration have normally been sold as pets. However, in the US I have seen dogs at shows, some of which were champions, with large white patching on their body. The use of dogs with too much white in their marking could be the first steps towards albinism, and even deafness. Concerned breeders will normally register such 'mis-marks,' but put an endorsement on the registration at The Kennel Club, to the effect that 'progeny are ineligible for registration.'

Size: Height: dogs: 61 cms (24 ins) and upwards; bitches: 56 cms (22 ins) and upwards. Type and symmetry of greatest importance, and on no account to be sacrificed to size alone.

While the standard has been slightly altered over time, it does not give an upper permissible size, thus giving leeway for increasing sizes to be produced and exhibited with success. While these larger dogs may be very eye-catching, it would be a sad day if a good, smaller specimen was ignored by a judge who felt that one who was larger would look more spectacular in the Group competition. 'Bigger' is not always 'better'! Modern, balanced diets will surely have contributed to the increased size of puppies, rather along the lines that human children appear to be a little larger in every generation. Overall balance is very important and should be a prime concern.

Faults: Any departure from the foregoing points should be considered a fault and the seriousness with which the fault should be regarded should be in exact proportion to its degree.

Note: Male animals should have two apparently normal testicles fully descended into the scrotum.

OLD ENGLISH SHEEPDOG

Knowing the characteristics of the breed will surely help when making this very important decision. A well-reared puppy is a joy to own. Therefore, prospective owners should make contact with caring and informed breeders, who will be honest, helpful, and reliable for advice throughout the animal's life. The best contact is by personal recommendation. It may be that your local canine society may know of someone involved in the breed in your own locality. If no personal recommendation is available, then contact The Kennel Club, for they can readily furnish you with the details of the secretary of the regional club that is nearest to you. Don't expect to find puppies ready and waiting for sale, as many breeders will have only an occasional litter, but if they are caring and honest, then it is worth waiting until they can sell you a quality pup.

Unless you have had previous experience, you should take time to learn all you can about the needs of a breed, well before you make a purchase. All too frequently people will see a picture and decide that is the breed they want! With few exceptions, puppies can be located and quickly purchased, from such sources as running advertisements in local papers, offering multiple breeds, or from commercial publications that will sell anything from a table to a car or puppy. Included in their listings will surely be 'pets and livestock.' Respectable breeders will only sell to those who have owned one of the breed, or to those who have literally been 'interrogated' as to what facilities and time they can devote to the new addition to their household. Sometimes this may involve a visit to the prospective new home, followed by further interviewing when all possible early advice is conveyed. Breeders who are totally honest and upright will wish to ensure that a new home is suitable, and the owners aware of the time and attention required. Prospective owners should not, therefore, resent any breeder wishing to go through these procedures, before allowing one of their carefully bred and reared puppies to go to a new owner. It is now also becoming acceptable that new owners will sign an agreement, that if for any reason whatsoever they are unable to keep their puppy, they will contact the breeder.

What do we expect to find in our Bobtail? We can hope for a happy and amenable animal who will readily fit in with your home and domestic routine. As with children, the Bobtail will respond well to a certain routine, and loving, consistent discipline. As long as they learn just what they are, and are not, allowed to do quite early in life, they will respond with affection and obedience. Never forget that the breed was used as a drover's working animal, so it will therefore need a certain amount of regular exercise. The pretty, cuddly puppy will not remain small for long, and with increased growth will require certain changes in the daily routine.

COMMITMENT OF OWNERSHIP

You have chosen a Bobtail, which means that you have decided which characteristics you want in a dog and what type of dog will best fit into your family and lifestyle. If you have selected a breeder, you

BREEDER'S BLUEPRINT

If you are considering breeding your bitch, it is very important that you are familiar with the breed standard. Reputable

breeders breed with the intention of producing dogs that are as close as possible to the standard, and contribute to the advancement of the breed. Study the standard for both physical appearance and temperament, and make certain your bitch and your chosen stud dog measure up.

Unfortunately, when a puppy is bought by someone who does not take into consideration the time and attention that dog ownership requires, it is the puppy who suffers when he is either abandoned or placed in a shelter by a frustrated owner. So all of the 'homework' you do in preparation for your pup's arrival will benefit you both. The more informed you are, the more you will know what to expect and the better equipped you will be to

handle the ups and downs of raising a puppy. Hopefully, everyone in the household is willing to do his part in raising and caring for the pup. The anticipation of owning a dog often brings a lot of promises from excited family members: 'I will walk him every day,' 'I will feed him,' 'I will housebreak him,' etc., but these things take time and effort, and promises can easily be forgotten once the novelty of the new pet has worn off.

have gone a step further—you have done your research and found a responsible, conscientious person who breeds quality Bobtails and who should be a reliable source of help as you and your puppy adjust to life together. If you have observed a litter in action, you have obtained a firsthand look at the dynamics of a puppy 'pack' and, thus, you should learn about each pup's individual personality—perhaps you have even found one that particularly appeals to you.

However, even if you have not yet found the Bobtail puppy of your dreams, observing pups will help you learn to recognise certain behaviour and to determine what a pup's behaviour indicates about his temperament. You will be able to pick out which pups are the leaders, which ones are less outgoing, which ones are confident, which ones are shy, playful, friendly, aggressive, etc. Equally as important, you will learn to recognise what a healthy pup should look and act like. All of these things will help you in your search, and when you find the Bobtail that was meant for you, you will know it!

Researching your breed, selecting a responsible breeder and observing as many pups as possible are all important steps on the way to dog ownership. It may seem like a lot of effort…and you have not even taken the pup home yet! Remember, though, you cannot be too careful when it comes to deciding on the type of dog you want and finding out about your prospective pup's background. Buying a puppy is not—or should not be—just another whimsical purchase. This is one instance in which you actually do get to choose your own family! You may be thinking that buying a puppy should be fun—it should not be so serious and so much work. Keep in mind that your puppy is not a cuddly stuffed toy or decorative lawn ornament, but a creature that will become a real member of your family. You will come to realise that, whilst buying a puppy is a pleasurable and exciting endeavour, it is not something to be taken lightly. Relax…the fun will start when the pup comes home!

Always keep in mind that a puppy is nothing more than a baby in a furry disguise…a baby who is virtually helpless in a human world and who trusts his owner for fulfilment of his basic needs for survival. In addition to water and shelter, your pup needs care, protection, guidance and love. If you are not prepared to commit to this, then you are not prepared to own a dog.

Wait a minute, you say. How hard could this be? All of my neighbours own dogs and they seem to be doing just fine. Why should I have to worry about all of this? Well, you should not worry about it; in fact, you will probably find that once your Bobtail pup gets used to his new home, he will fall into his place in the family quite naturally. But it never hurts to emphasise the commitment of dog ownership. With some time and patience, it is really not too difficult to raise a curious and exuberant Bobtail pup to be a well-adjusted and well-mannered adult dog—a dog that could be your most loyal friend.

PREPARING PUPPY'S PLACE IN YOUR HOME

Researching your breed and finding a breeder are only two aspects of the 'homework' you will have to do before bringing your Bobtail puppy home. You will also have to prepare your home and family for the new addition. Much as you would prepare a nursery for a newborn baby, you will need to designate a place in your home that will be the puppy's own. How you prepare your home will depend on how much freedom the dog will be allowed. Whatever you decide, you must ensure that he has a place that he can 'call his own.'

When you bring your new puppy into your home, you are bringing him into what will become his home as well. Obviously, you did not buy a puppy so that he could take over your house, but in order for a puppy to grow into a stable, well-adjusted dog, he has to feel comfortable in his surroundings. Remember, he is leaving the warmth and security of his mother and littermates, as well as the familiarity of the only place he has ever known, so it is important to make his transition as easy as possible. By preparing a place in your home for the puppy, you are making him feel as welcome as possible in a strange new place. It should not take him long to get used to it, but the sudden shock of being transplanted is somewhat traumatic for a young pup. Imagine how a small child would feel in the same situation—that is how your puppy must be feeling. It is up to you to reassure him and to let him know, 'Little chap, you are going to like it here!'

DID YOU KNOW?

Taking your dog from the breeder to your home in a car can be a very uncomfortable experience for both of you. The puppy will have been taken from his warm, friendly, safe environment and brought into a strange new environment. An environment that moves! Be prepared for loose bowels, urination, crying, whining and even fear biting. With proper love and encouragement when you arrive home, the stress of the trip should quickly disappear.

INFORMATION...

You should not even think about buying a puppy that looks sick, undernourished, overly frightened or nervous.

Sometimes a timid puppy will warm up to you after a 30-minute 'let's-get-acquainted' session.

WHAT YOU SHOULD BUY

CRATE

To someone unfamiliar with the use of crates in dog training, it may seem like punishment to shut a dog in a crate, but this is

Your local pet shop should have a wide assortment of crates. You need an extra large crate for a Bobtail.

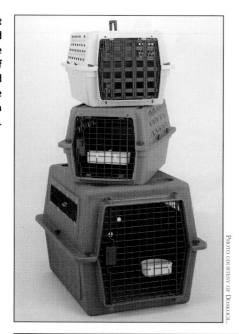

PHOTO COURTESY OF DOSKOCIL.

not the case at all. Although all breeders do not advocate crate training, more and more breeders and trainers are recommending crates as a preferred tool for show puppies as well as pet puppies. Crates are not cruel—crates have many humane and highly effective uses in dog care and training. For example, crate training is a very popular and very successful housebreaking method. A crate can keep your dog safe during travel and, perhaps most importantly, a crate provides your dog with a place of his own in your home. It serves as a 'doggie bedroom'

Wire crates are very popular because they are light, inexpensive, easily cleaned and easily disassembled for transport.

of sorts—your Bobtail can curl up in his crate when he wants to sleep or when he just needs a break. Many dogs sleep in their crates overnight. When lined with soft bedding and a favourite toy, a crate becomes a cosy pseudo-den for your dog. Like his ancestors, he too will seek out the comfort and retreat of a den—you just happen to be providing him with something a little more luxurious than his early ancestors enjoyed.

As far as purchasing a crate, the type that you buy is up to you. It will most likely be one of the two most popular types: wire or fibreglass. There are advantages and disadvantages to each type. For example, a wire crate is more open, allowing the air to flow through and affording the dog a view of what is going on around him whilst a fibreglass crate is sturdier. Both can double as travel crates, providing protection for the dog. The size of the crate is another thing to consider. Puppies do not stay puppies forever—in fact, sometimes it seems as if they grow right before your eyes. A small-sized crate may be fine for a very young Bobtail pup, but it will not do him much good for long! Unless you have the money and the inclination to buy a new crate every time your pup has a growth spurt, it is better to get

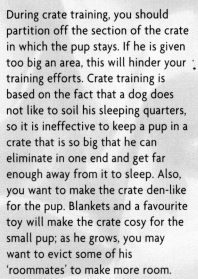

CRATE TRAINING TIPS

During crate training, you should partition off the section of the crate in which the pup stays. If he is given too big an area, this will hinder your training efforts. Crate training is based on the fact that a dog does not like to soil his sleeping quarters, so it is ineffective to keep a pup in a crate that is so big that he can eliminate in one end and get far enough away from it to sleep. Also, you want to make the crate den-like for the pup. Blankets and a favourite toy will make the crate cosy for the small pup; as he grows, you may want to evict some of his 'roommates' to make more room.

It will take some coaxing at first, but be patient. Given some time to get used to it, your pup will adapt to his new home-within-a-home quite nicely.

one that will accommodate your dog both as a pup and at full size. A medium-size crate will be necessary for a full-grown Bobtail, who stands approximately 21 inches high.

BEDDING

Veterinary bedding in the dog's crate will help the dog feel more at home and you may also like to pop in a small blanket. This will take the place of the leaves, twigs, etc., that the pup would use in the wild to make a den; the pup can make his own

frequently in case he has an accident in his crate, and replace or remove any blanket that becomes ragged and starts to fall apart.

Toys
Toys are a must for dogs of all ages, especially for curious playful pups. Puppies are the 'children' of the dog world, and what child does not love toys? Chew toys provide enjoyment for both dog and owner—your dog will enjoy playing with his favourite toys, whilst you will enjoy the fact that they distract him from your expensive shoes and leather sofa. Puppies love to chew; in fact, chewing is a physical need for pups as they are teething, and everything looks appetising! The full range of your possessions—from old

'burrow' in the crate. Although your pup is far removed from his den-making ancestors, the denning instinct is still a part of his genetic makeup. Second, until you bring your pup home, he has been sleeping amidst the warmth of his mother and litter-mates, and whilst a blanket is not the same as a warm, breathing body, it still provides heat and something with which to snuggle. You will want to wash your pup's bedding

HOW VACCINES WORK

If you've just bought a puppy, you surely know the importance of having your pup vaccinated, but do you understand how vaccines work? Vaccines contain the same bacteria or viruses that cause the disease you want to prevent, but they have been chemically modified so that they don't cause any harm. Instead, the vaccine causes your dog to produce antibodies that fight the harmful bacteria. Thus, if your pup is exposed to the disease in the future, the antibodies will destroy the viruses or bacteria.

tea towel to Oriental carpet—are fair game in the teeth of an eyeing pup. Puppies are not all that discerning when it comes to finding something to literally 'sink their teeth into'—everything tastes great!

Bobtail puppies are fairly aggressive chewers and only the hardest, strongest toys should be offered to them. Breeders advise owners to resist stuffed toys, because they can become de-stuffed in no time. The overly excited pup may ingest the stuffing, which is neither digestible nor nutritious.

Similarly, squeaky toys are quite popular, but must be avoided for the Bobtail. Perhaps a squeaky toy can be used as an aid in training, but not for free play. If a pup 'disembowels' one of these, the small plastic squeaker inside can be dangerous if swallowed. Monitor the condition of all your pup's toys carefully and get rid of any that have been chewed to the point of becoming potentially dangerous.

Be careful of natural bones, which have a tendency to splinter into sharp, dangerous pieces. Also be careful of

PUPPY PERSONALITY

When a litter becomes available to you, choosing a pup out of all those adorable faces will not be an easy task! Sound

temperament is of utmost importance, but each pup has its own personality and some may be better suited to you than others. A feisty, independent pup will do well in a home with older children and adults, whilst quiet, shy puppies will thrive in a home with minimum noise and distractions. Your breeder knows the pups best and should be able to guide you in the right direction.

TOYS, TOYS, TOYS!

With a big variety of dog toys available, and so many that look like they would be a lot of fun for a dog, be careful in your selection. It is amazing what a set of puppy teeth can do to an innocent-looking toy, so, obviously, safety is a major consideration. Be sure to choose the most durable products that you can find. Hard nylon bones and toys are a safe bet, and many of them are offered in different scents and

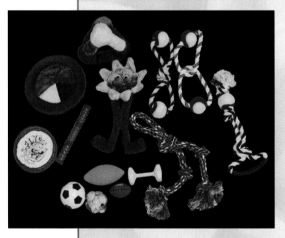

flavours that will be sure to capture your dog's attention. It is always fun to play a game of catch with your dog, and there are balls and flying discs that are specially made to withstand dog teeth.

rawhide, which can turn into pieces that are easy to swallow and become a mushy mess on your carpet.

LEAD

A nylon lead is probably the best option as it is the most resistant to puppy teeth should your pup take a liking to chewing on his lead. Of course, this is a habit that should be nipped in the bud, but if your pup likes to chew on his lead he has a very slim chance of being able to chew through the strong nylon. Nylon leads are also lightweight, which is good for a young Bobtail who is just getting used to the idea of walking on a lead. For everyday walking and safety purposes, the nylon lead is a good choice. As your pup grows up and gets used to walking on the lead, you may want to purchase a flexible lead. These leads allow you to extend the length to give the dog a broader area to explore or to shorten the length to keep the dog near you. Of course there are special leads for training purposes, such as

MENTAL AND DENTAL

Toys not only help your puppy get the physical and mental stimulation he needs but also provide a great way to keep his teeth clean. Hard rubber or nylon toys, especially those constructed with grooves, are designed to scrape away plaque, preventing bad breath and gum infection.

headcollars, and specially made leather harnesses, but these are not necessary for routine walks.

COLLAR

Your pup should get used to wearing a collar all the time since you will want to attach his ID tags to it. You have to attach the lead to something! A lightweight nylon collar is a good choice; make sure that it fits snugly enough so that the pup cannot wriggle out of it, but is loose enough so that it will not be uncomfortably tight around the pup's neck. You should be able to fit a finger between the pup and the collar. It may take some time for your pup to get used to wearing the collar, but soon he will not even notice that it is there. Choke collars are made for training, but should only be used by an experienced handler.

FOOD AND WATER BOWLS

Your pup will need two bowls, one for food and one for water. You may want two sets of bowls, one for inside and one for outside, depending on where the dog will be fed and where he will be spending time. Stainless steel or sturdy plastic bowls are popular choices. Plastic bowls are more chewable. Dogs tend not to chew on the steel variety, which can be sterilised. It is important to buy sturdy bowls since anything is in danger of being chewed by puppy teeth and you

DO YOUR HOMEWORK!

In order to know whether or not a puppy will fit into your lifestyle, you need to assess his personality. A good

way to do this is to interact with his parents. Your pup inherits not only his appearance but also his personality and temperament from the sire and dam. If the parents are fearful or overly aggressive, these same traits may likely show up in your puppy.

Your local pet shop will have a suitable selection of leads and collars from which you can choose appropriate equipment for the size of your dog.

will find out what else you need as you go along—grooming supplies, flea/tick protection, baby gates to partition a room, etc. These things will vary depending on your situation but it is important that you have everything you need to feed and make your Bobtail comfortable in his first few days at home.

do not want your dog to be constantly chewing apart his bowl (for his safety and for your purse!).

CLEANING SUPPLIES

Until your pup is housetrained, you will be doing a lot of cleaning. Accidents will occur, which is acceptable in the beginning because the puppy does not know any better. All you can do is be prepared to clean up any 'accidents.' Old rags, towels, newspapers and a safe disinfectant are good to have on hand.

BEYOND THE BASICS

The items previously discussed are the bare necessities. You

DOCUMENTATION

Two important documents you will get from the breeder are the pup's pedigree and registration certificate. The breeder should register the litter and each pup with The Kennel Club, and it is necessary for you to have the paperwork if you plan on showing or breeding in the future.

Make sure you know the breeder's intentions on which type of registration he will obtain for the pup. There are limited registrations which may prohibit the dog from being shown, bred or from competing in non-conformation trials such as Working or Agility if the breeder feels that the pup is not of sufficient quality to do so. There is also a type of registration that will permit the dog in non-conformation competition only.

On the reverse side of the registration certificate, the new owner can find the transfer section which must be signed by the breeder.

The **BUCKLE COLLAR** is the standard collar used for everyday purpose. Be sure that you adjust the buckle on growing puppies. Check it every day. It can become too tight overnight! These collars can be made of leather or nylon. Attach your dog's identification tags to this collar.

The **CHOKE COLLAR** is the usual collar recommended for training. It is constructed of highly polished steel so that it slides easily through the stainless steel loop. The idea is that the dog controls the pressure around its neck and he will stop pulling if the collar becomes uncomfortable. Never leave a choke collar on your dog when not training.

The **HALTER** is for a trained dog that has to be restrained to prevent running away, chasing a cat and the like. Considered the most humane of all collars, it is frequently used on smaller dogs for which collars are not comfortable.

You can choose from a large assortment of light plastic, heavy plastic, pottery and stainless steel water and food bowls for your Bobtail.

PUPPY-PROOFING YOUR HOME

Aside from making sure that your Bobtail will be comfortable in your home, you also have to make sure that your home is safe for your Bobtail. This means taking precautions that your pup will not get into anything he should not get into and that there is nothing within his reach that may harm him should he sniff it, chew it, inspect it, etc. This probably

seems obvious since, whilst you are primarily concerned with your pup's safety, at the same time you do not want your belongings to be ruined. Breakables should be placed out of reach if your dog is to have full run of the house. If he is to be limited to certain places within the house, keep any potentially dangerous items in the 'off-limits' areas. An electrical cord can pose a danger should the puppy decide to taste it—and who is going to convince a pup that it would not make a great chew toy? Cords should be fastened tightly against the wall. If your dog is going to spend time in a crate, make sure that there is nothing near his crate that he can reach if he sticks his curious little nose or paws through the openings. Just as you would with a child, keep all household cleaners and chemicals where the pup cannot reach them.

It is also important to make sure that the outside of your home is safe. Of course your puppy should never be unsupervised, but a pup let loose in the garden will want to run and explore, and he should be granted that freedom. Do not let a fence give you a false sense of security; you would be

It is your responsibility to clean up after your dog has relieved himself. Pet shops have various aids to assist in the cleanup job.

INSURANCE

Many good breeders will offer you insurance with your new puppy, which is an excellent idea. The first few weeks of insurance will probably be covered free of charge or with only minimal cost, allowing you to take up the policy when this expires. If you own a pet dog, it is sensible to take out such a policy as veterinary fees can be high, although routine vaccinations and boosters are not covered. Look carefully at the many options open to you before deciding which suits you best.

surprised how crafty (and persistent) a dog can be in learning how to dig under and squeeze his way through small holes, or to jump or climb over a fence. The remedy is to make the fence well embedded into the ground and high enough so that it really is impossible for your dog to get over it (about 3 metres should suffice). Be sure to repair or secure any gaps in the fence. Check the fence periodically to ensure that it is in good shape and make repairs as needed; a very determined pup may return to the same

49

DID YOU KNOW?

It will take at least two weeks for your puppy to become accustomed to his new surroundings. Give him lots of love, attention, handling, frequent opportunities to relieve himself, a diet he likes to eat and a place he can call his own.

up a schedule for the pup's vaccinations; the breeder will inform you of which ones the pup has already received and the vet can continue from there.

INTRODUCTION TO THE FAMILY

Everyone in the house will be excited about the puppy coming

spot to 'work on it' until he is able to get through.

FIRST TRIP TO THE VET

You have picked out your puppy, and your home and family are ready. Now all you have to do is collect your Bobtail from the breeder and the fun begins, right? Well...not so fast. Something else you need to prepare is your pup's first trip to the veterinary surgeon. Perhaps the breeder can recommend someone in the area that specialises in Bobtails, or maybe you know some other Bobtail owners who can suggest a good vet. Either way, you should have an appointment arranged for your pup before you pick him up and plan on taking him for an examination before bringing him home.

The pup's first visit will consist of an overall examina-tion to make sure that the pup does not have any problems that are not apparent to the eye. The veterinary surgeon will also set

NATURAL TOXINS

Examine your grass and garden landscaping before bringing your puppy home. Many varieties of plants have leaves, stems or flowers that are toxic if ingested, and you

can depend on a curious puppy to investigate them. Ask your vet for information on poisonous plants or research them at your library.

home and will want to pet him and play with him, but it is best to make the introduction low-key so as not to overwhelm the puppy. He is apprehensive already. It is the first time he has been separated from his mother and the breeder, and the ride to your home is likely to be the first time he has been in a car. The last thing you want to do is smother him, as this will only frighten him further. This is not to say that human contact is not extremely necessary at this stage, because this is the time when a connection between the pup and his human family is formed. Gentle petting and soothing words should help console him, as well as just putting him down and letting him explore on his own (under your watchful eye, of course).

The pup may approach the family members or may busy himself with exploring for a while. Gradually, each person should spend some time with

TOXIC PLANTS

Many plants can be toxic to dogs. If you see your dog carrying a piece of vegetation in his mouth, approach

him in a quiet, disinterested manner, avoid eye contact, pet him and gradually remove the plant from his mouth. Alternatively, offer him a treat and maybe he'll drop the plant on his own accord. Be sure no toxic plants are growing in your own garden.

CHEMICAL TOXINS

Scour your garage for potential puppy dangers. Remove weed killers, pesticides and antifreeze materials. Antifreeze is highly toxic and even a few drops can kill an adult dog. The sweet taste attracts the animal, who will quickly consume it from the floor or curbside.

the pup, one at a time, crouching down to get as close to the pup's level as possible and letting him sniff his hands and petting him gently. He definitely needs human attention and he needs to be touched—this is how to form an immediate bond. Just remember that the pup is experiencing a lot of things for

51

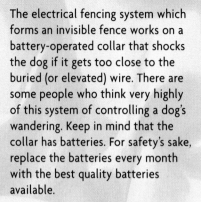

ELECTRICAL FENCING

The electrical fencing system which forms an invisible fence works on a battery-operated collar that shocks the dog if it gets too close to the buried (or elevated) wire. There are some people who think very highly of this system of controlling a dog's wandering. Keep in mind that the collar has batteries. For safety's sake, replace the batteries every month with the best quality batteries available.

the first time, at the same time. There are new people, new noises, new smells, and new things to investigate: so be gentle, be affectionate, and be as comforting as you can be.

PUP'S FIRST NIGHT HOME

You have travelled home with your new charge safely in his crate. He's been to the vet for a thorough check-up; he's been weighed, his papers examined; perhaps he's even been vaccinated and wormed as well. He's met the family, licked the whole family, including the excited children and the less-than-happy cat. He's explored his area, his new bed, the garden and anywhere else he's been permitted. He's eaten his first meal at home and relieved himself in the proper place. He's heard lots of new sounds,

smelled new friends and seen more of the outside world than ever before.

That was just the first day! He's worn out and is ready for bed...or so you think!

It's puppy's first night and you are ready to say 'Good night'—keep in mind that this is puppy's first night ever to be sleeping alone. His dam and littermates are no longer at paw's length and he's a bit scared, cold and lonely. Be reassuring to your new family member. This is not the time to spoil him and give in to his inevitable whining.

Puppies whine. They whine to let others know where they are and hopefully to get company out of it. Place your pup in his new bed or crate in his room and close the door. Mercifully, he may fall asleep without a peep. If the inevitable occurs, ignore the whining: he is fine. Be strong and keep his

PUPPY-PROOFING

Thoroughly puppy-proof your house before bringing your puppy home. Never use roach or rodent poisons in any area accessible to the puppy. Avoid the use of toilet cleaners. Most dogs are born with 'toilet sonar' and will take a drink if the lid is left open. Also keep the rubbish secured and out of reach.

Socialisation is an important feature in your dog's training. The new puppy should meet all members of the family, neighbours and other dogs.

interest in mind. Do not allow yourself to feel guilty and visit the pup. He will fall asleep eventually.

Many breeders recommend placing a piece of bedding from his former home in his new bed so that he recognises the scent of his littermates. Others still advise placing a hot water bottle in his bed for warmth. This latter may be a good idea provided the pup doesn't attempt to suckle—he'll get good and wet and may not fall asleep so fast.

Puppy's first night can be somewhat stressful for the pup and his new family. Remember that you are setting the tone of nighttime at your house. Unless you want to play with your pup every evening at 10 p.m., midnight and 2 a.m., don't initiate the habit. Your family will thank you, and so will your pup!

DID YOU KNOW?

Some experts in canine health advise that stress during a dog's early years of development can compromise and weaken his immune system and may trigger the potential for a shortened life expectancy. They emphasise the need for happy and stress-free growing-up years.

53

INFORMATION...

You will probably start feeding your pup the same food that he has been getting from the breeder; the breeder should give you a few days' supply to start you off. Although you should not give your pup too many treats, you will want to have puppy

treats on hand for coaxing, training, rewards, etc. Be careful, though, as a small pup's calorie requirements are relatively low and a few treats can add up to almost a full day's worth of calories without the required nutrition.

PREVENTING PUPPY PROBLEMS

SOCIALISATION
Now that you have done all of the preparatory work and have helped your pup get accustomed to his new home and family, it is about time for you to have some fun! Socialising your Bobtail pup gives you the opportunity to show off your new friend, and your pup gets to reap the benefits of being an adorable furry creature that people will want to pet and, in general, think is absolutely precious!

Besides getting to know his new family, your puppy should be exposed to other people, animals and situations, but of course he must not come into close contact with dogs you don't know well until his course of injections is fully complete. This will help him become well adjusted as he grows up and less prone to being timid or fearful of the new things he will encounter. Your pup's socialisation began at the breeder's but now it is your responsibility to continue

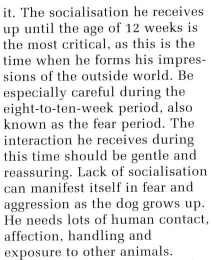

it. The socialisation he receives up until the age of 12 weeks is the most critical, as this is the time when he forms his impressions of the outside world. Be especially careful during the eight-to-ten-week period, also known as the fear period. The interaction he receives during this time should be gentle and reassuring. Lack of socialisation can manifest itself in fear and aggression as the dog grows up. He needs lots of human contact, affection, handling and exposure to other animals.

Once your pup has received his necessary vaccinations, feel free to take him out and about (on his lead, of course). Walk him around the neighbourhood, take him on your daily errands, let people pet him, let him meet other dogs and pets, etc. Puppies do not have to try to make friends; there will be no shortage of people who will

FINANCIAL RESPONSIBILITY

Grooming tools, collars, leashes, dog beds and, of course, toys will be an expense to you when you first obtain your pup, and the cost will continue throughout your dog's lifetime. If your puppy damages or destroys your possessions (as most puppies surely will!) or something belonging to a neighbour, you can calculate additional expense. There is also flea and pest control, which every dog owner faces more than once. You must be able to handle the financial responsibility of owning a dog.

SOCIALISATION

Thorough socialisation includes not only meeting new people but also being introduced to new experiences such as riding in the car, having his coat brushed, hearing the television, walking in a crowd—the list is endless. The more your pup experiences, and the more positive the experiences are, the less of a shock and the less scary it will be for your pup to encounter new things.

want to introduce themselves. Just make sure that you carefully supervise each meeting. If the neighbourhood children want to say hello, for example, that is great—children and pups most often make great companions. Sometimes an excited child can unintentionally handle a pup too roughly, or an overzealous pup can playfully nip a little too hard. You want to make socialisation experiences positive ones. What a pup learns during this very formative stage will affect his attitude toward future encounters. You want your dog to be comfortable around everyone. A pup that has a bad experience with a child may grow up to be

MANNERS MATTER

During the socialisation process, a puppy should meet people, experience different environments and definitely be exposed to other canines. Through playing and interacting with other dogs, your puppy will learn lessons, ranging from controlling the pressure of his jaws by biting his litter mates to the inner-workings of the canine pack that he will apply to his human relationships for the rest of his life. That is why removing a puppy from its litter too early (before eight weeks) can be detrimental to the pup's development.

a dog that is shy around or aggressive toward children.

CONSISTENCY IN TRAINING

Dogs, being pack animals, naturally need a leader, or else they try to establish dominance in their packs. When you bring a dog into your family, the choice of who becomes the leader and who becomes the 'pack' is entirely up to you! Your pup's intuitive quest for dominance, coupled with the fact that it is nearly impossible to look at an adorable Bobtail pup, with his 'puppy-dog' eyes and his too-big-for-his-head-floppy ears, and not cave in, give the pup almost an unfair advantage in getting the upper hand! A pup will definitely test the waters to see what he can and cannot do. Do not give in to those pleading eyes—stand your ground when it comes to disciplining the pup and make sure that all family members do the same. It will only confuse the pup when Mother tells him to get off the sofa when he is used to sitting up there with Father to watch the nightly news. Avoid discrepancies by having all members of the household decide on the rules before the pup even comes home...and be consistent in enforcing them! Early training shapes the dog's personality, so you cannot be unclear in what you expect.

COMMON PUPPY PROBLEMS

The best way to prevent puppy problems is to be proactive in stopping an undesirable behaviour as soon as it starts.

DID YOU KNOW?

Breeders rarely release puppies until they are eight to ten weeks of age. This is an acceptable age for most breeds of dog, excepting toy breeds, which are not released until around 12 weeks, given their petite sizes. If a breeder has a puppy that is 12 weeks or more, it is likely well socialised and housetrained. Be sure that it is otherwise healthy before deciding to take it home.

The old saying 'You can't teach an old dog new tricks' does not necessarily hold true, but it is true that it is much easier to discourage bad behaviour in a young developing pup than to wait until the pup's bad behaviour becomes the adult dog's bad habit. There are some problems that are especially prevalent in puppies as they develop.

NIPPING

As puppies start to teethe, they feel the need to sink their teeth into anything available... unfortunately that includes your fingers, arms, hair and toes. You may find this behaviour cute for the first five seconds...until you feel just how sharp those puppy teeth are. This is something you want to discourage immediately and consistently with a firm 'No!' (or whatever number of firm 'No's' it takes for him to understand that you mean business). Then replace your finger with an appropriate chew toy. Whilst this behaviour is merely annoying when the dog is young, it can become dangerous as your Bobtail's adult teeth grow in and his jaws develop, and he continues to think it is okay to gnaw on human appendages. Your Bobtail does not mean any harm with a friendly nip, but he also does not know his own strength.

CRYING/WHINING

Your pup will often cry, whine, whimper, howl or make some type of commotion when he is left alone. This is basically his way of calling out for attention to make sure that you know he is there and that you have not forgotten about him. He feels insecure when he is left alone, when you are out of the house and he is in his crate or when you are in another part of the house and he cannot see you. The noise he is making is an expression of the anxiety he feels at being alone, so he needs to be taught that being alone is okay. You are not actually training the dog to stop making noise, you are training him to feel comfortable when he is alone and thus removing the need for him to make the noise.

TRAINING TIP

Training your puppy takes much patience and can be frustrating at times, but you should see results from your efforts. If you have a puppy that seems untrainable, take him to a trainer or behaviourist. The dog may have a personality problem that requires the help of a professional, or perhaps you need help in learning how to train your dog.

A curious Bobtail on the move... Crate training eliminates the possible dangers your young Bobtail can encounter when you cannot be around to supervise.

This is where the crate filled with cosy bedding and a toy comes in handy. You want to know that he is safe when you are not there to supervise, and you know that he will be safe in his crate rather than roaming freely about the house. In order for the pup to stay in his crate without making a fuss, he needs to be comfortable in his crate. On that note, it is extremely important that the crate is never used as a form of punishment, or the pup will have a negative association with the crate.

Accustom the pup to the crate in short, gradually increasing time intervals in which you put him in the crate, maybe with a treat, and stay in the room with him. If he cries or makes a fuss, do not go to him, but stay in his sight. Gradually he will realise that staying in his crate is all right without your help, and it will not be so traumatic for him when you are not around. You may want to leave the radio on softly when you leave the house; the sound of human voices may be comforting to him.

59

FEEDING YOUR BOBTAIL

When you take your puppy home, it is normally around eight weeks of age, should have been carefully weaned and will perhaps be on three meals per day. Whether or not you fully agree with the breeder's diet and feeding regimen, it is inadvisable to make sudden changes. After all, it will not have been so long since your puppy was feeding from its mother and will only have been weaned for perhaps three weeks. Your breeder will know which food is best suited and how much is needed. If, at some time, you need or decide to make changes in the pup's diet, then the change should always be administered with the greatest care, and without haste. It is essential that new owners maintain contact with their breeder, and my advice is that before any great alterations in routine and/or diet, they should first consult with those more experienced. It is normal practice for caring breeders to advise on all aspects of the puppy's lifestyle, and they will invariably let you know what food to obtain beforehand. Some breeders will actually ensure that there is some ready for you to take home. In days gone by, when plenty of fresh meat was obtainable at reasonable prices, we would normally feed that, mixed with some good-quality biscuit meal. In more recent times, with restrictions on the productions and retailing of fresh meat, more dog owners have moved over to the complete foods, while some prefer tins. The former comes in flake or pellet form. My personal preference is that it is fed moistened. If a dog was living wild, the food that it hunted would not be in a dry

> ### DID YOU KNOW?
>
> A good test for proper diet is the colour, odour and firmness of your dog's stool. A healthy dog usually produces three semi-hard stools per day. The stools should have no unpleasant odour. They should be the same colour from excretion to excretion.

form, therefore I feel it is unfair to expect our dogs' digestions to adapt to unnatural nutrition.

When considering the purchase of any breed, the cost of feeding is something that should be taken into account. A growing dog will gradually need larger quantities, even though the number of feedings will eventually reduce to one per day. We always fed our puppies a cereal-type breakfast, a light lunch and an evening meat-and-meal mixture. Gradually, the breakfast was reduced in quantity, as was the mid-day feeding, while the evening meal was gradually increased. The middle meal was the first to be discontinued, followed by the breakfast. The modern, complete foods are carefully formulated and will be graded according to needs: puppy, junior, adult, senior, etc. They are sold with details of amounts required according to

DID YOU KNOW?

You must store your dried dog food carefully. Open packages of dog food quickly lose their vitamin value, usually within 90 days of being opened. Mould spores and vermin could also contaminate the food.

size of breed and any preparation needs. The grading ensures that the balance of protein and carbohydrates are in keeping with growth stages. Again, other necessary vitamin and mineral requirements should be adequately covered in the formula.

Having owned, bred and exhibited Bobtails for over 25 years, we found that the breed does not easily accept sudden diet changes or breaks in routine. Dogs don't get bored with the same food served 7 days a week for 52 weeks a year, as a human would. My own experience with changes in feeding patterns, just to give more variety, can soon lead to upset digestion, and the resulting dirty rear end! As a worker a century ago, the

DID YOU KNOW?

The cost of food must also be mentioned. All dogs need a good quality food with an adequate supply of protein to develop their bones and muscles properly. Most dogs are not picky eaters but unless fed properly they can quickly succumb to skin problems.

FOOD PREFERENCE

Selecting the best dried dog food is difficult. There is no majority consensus amongst veterinary scientists as to the value of nutrient analyses (protein, fat, fibre, moisture, ash, cholesterol, minerals, etc.). All agree that feeding trials are what matters, but you also have to consider the individual dog. Its weight, age, activity and what pleases its taste, all must be considered. It is probably best to take the advice of your veterinary surgeon. Every dog's dietary requirements vary, even during the lifetime of a particular dog.

If your dog is fed a good dried food, it does not require supplements of meat or vegetables. Dogs do appreciate a little variety in their diets so you may choose to stay with the same brand, but vary the flavour. Alternatively you may wish to add a little flavoured stock to give a difference to the taste.

Bobtail would certainly not have been fed a protein-rich diet. Though we need more for our growing puppy, experience has shown that some 18–20% protein was sufficient for our adult dogs. If digestion is upset, then near-starvation for 24 hours, followed by gradual and light restoration of meals will usually suffice. The first food after such an upset would perhaps be a little scrambled egg and perhaps a little white fish, which has been carefully checked to ensure there are no bones. These can then be gradually increased by a little of the normal diet, until all is well again. If this does not work, then you should consult your vet without delay, for animals can soon dehydrate and lose condition.

When selecting your dog's diet, three stages of development must be considered: the puppy stage, adult stage and the senior or veteran stage.

PUPPY STAGE

Puppies instinctively want to suck milk from their mother's teats and a normal puppy will exhibit this behaviour from just a few moments following birth. If puppies do not attempt to suckle within the first half-hour or so, they should be encouraged to do so by placing them on the nipples, having selected ones with plenty of milk. This early milk supply is important in providing colostrum to protect the puppies during the first eight to ten weeks of their lives. Although a mother's milk is much better than any milk formula, despite there being some excellent ones available, if the puppies do not feed you will have to feed them yourself.

For those with less experience, advice from a veterinary surgeon is important so that you feed not only the right quantity of milk but that of correct quality, fed at suitably frequent intervals, usually every two hours during the first few days of life.

Puppies should be allowed to nurse from their mothers for about the first six weeks, although from the third or fourth week you will have begun to introduce small portions of suitable solid food. Most breeders like to introduce alternate milk and meat meals initially, building up to weaning time.

By the time the puppies are seven or a maximum of eight weeks old, they should be fully weaned and fed solely on a proprietary puppy food. Selection of the most suitable, good-quality diet at this time is essential for a puppy's fastest growth rate is during the first year of life. Veterinary surgeons are usually able to offer advice in this regard and, although the frequency of meals will have been reduced over time, only when a young dog has reached the age of about 12 months should an adult diet be fed.

Puppy and junior diets should be well balanced for the needs of your dog, so that except in certain circumstances

DO DOGS HAVE TASTE BUDS?

Watching a dog 'wolf' or gobble his food, seemingly without chewing, leads an owner to wonder whether their dogs can taste anything. Yes,

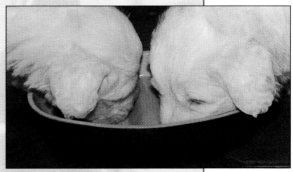

dogs have taste buds, with sensory perception of sweet, salty and sour. Puppies are born with fully mature taste buds.

additional vitamins, minerals and proteins will not be required.

ADULT DIETS

A dog is considered an adult when it has stopped growing, so in general the diet of a Bobtail can be changed to an adult one at about 10 to 12 months of age. Again you should rely upon your veterinary surgeon or dietary specialist to recommend an acceptable maintenance diet. Major dog food manufacturers specialise in this type of food,

What are you feeding your dog?

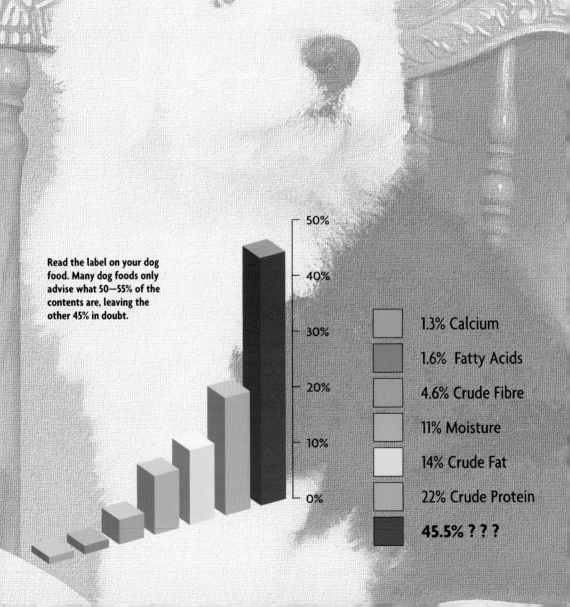

Read the label on your dog food. Many dog foods only advise what 50—55% of the contents are, leaving the other 45% in doubt.

50%

40%

30%

20%

10%

0%

1.3% Calcium

1.6% Fatty Acids

4.6% Crude Fibre

11% Moisture

14% Crude Fat

22% Crude Protein

45.5% ? ? ?

and it is merely necessary for you to select the one best suited to your dog's needs. Active dogs may have different requirements than sedate dogs.

SENIOR DIETS

As dogs get older, their metabolism changes. The older dog usually exercises less, moves more slowly and sleeps more. This change in lifestyle and physiological performance requires a change in diet. Since these changes take place slowly, they might not be recognisable. What is easily recognisable is weight gain. By continuing to feed your dog an adult-maintenance diet when it is slowing down metabolically, your dog will gain weight. Obesity in an older dog compounds the health problems that already accompany old age.

As your dog gets older, few of their organs function up to par. The kidneys slow down and the intestines become less efficient. These age-related factors are best handled with a change in diet and a change in feeding schedule to give smaller portions that are more easily digested.

There is no single best diet for every older dog. While many dogs do well on light or senior diets, other dogs do better on puppy diets or other special premium diets such as lamb and rice. Be sensitive to your senior Bobtail's diet and this will help control other problems that may arise with your old friend.

WATER

Just as your dog needs proper nutrition from his food, water is an essential 'nutrient' as well. Water keeps the dog's body properly hydrated and promotes normal function of the body's systems. During

'DOES THIS COLLAR MAKE ME LOOK FAT?'

Whilst humans may obsess about how they look and how trim their bodies are, many people believe that extra weight on their dogs is a good thing. The truth is, pets should not be over- or under-weight, as both can lead to or signal sickness. In order to tell how fit your pet is, run your hands over his ribs. Are his ribs buried under a layer of fat or are they sticking out considerably? If your pet is within his normal weight range, you should be able to feel the ribs easily. If you stand above him, the outline of his body should resemble an hourglass. Some breeds do tend to be leaner; while some are a bit stockier, but making sure your dog is the right weight for his breed will certainly contribute to his good health.

DRINK, DRANK, DRUNK— MAKE IT A DOUBLE

In both humans and dogs, as well as most living organisms, water forms the major part of nearly every body tissues. Naturally, we take water for granted, but without it, life as we know it would cease.

For dogs, water is needed to keep their bodies functioning biochemi-

cally. Additionally, water is needed to replace the water lost while panting. Unlike humans who are able to sweat to dissipate heat, dogs must pant to cool down, thereby losing the vital water from their bodies needed to regulate their body temperatures. Humans lose electrolyte-containing products and other body-fluid components through sweating; dogs do not lose anything except water. Water is essential always, but especially so when the weather is hot or humid or when your dog is exercising or working vigorously.

TIPPING THE SCALES

Good nutrition is vital to your dog's health, but many people end up over-feeding or giving unnecessary supplements. Here are some common doggie diet don'ts:
• Adding milk, yoghurt and cheese to your dog's diet may seem like a good idea for coat and skin care, but dairy products are very fattening and can cause indigestion.
• Diets high in fat will not cause heart attacks in dogs but will certainly cause your dog to gain weight.
• Most importantly, don't assume your dog will simply stop eating once he doesn't need any more food. Given the chance, he will eat you out of house and home!

housebreaking it is necessary to keep an eye on how much water your Bobtail is drinking, but once he is reliably trained he should have access to clean fresh water at all times, especially if you feed dried food. Make sure that the dog's water bowl is clean, and change the water often.

EXERCISE
As the Old English Sheepdog derives from the active, hardy droving dogs of yore, the breed requires more activity than most other dogs. Even though the Bobtail looks perfectly

contented napping by the hearth, he needs daily physical stimulation to maintain his condition. All dogs require some form of exercise, regardless of breed.

Regular walks, play sessions in the garden and letting the dog run free in the garden under your supervision are sufficient forms of exercise for the Bobtail. For those who are more ambitious, you will find that your Bobtail also enjoys long walks, an occasional hike or even a swim! Bear in mind that an overweight dog should never be suddenly over-exercised; instead he should be encouraged to increase exercise slowly.

Not only is exercise essential to keep the dog's body

CHANGE IN DIET

As your dog's caretaker, you know the importance of keeping his diet consistent, but sometimes when you run out of food or if you're on holiday, you have to make a change quickly. Some dogs will experience digestive problems but most will not. If you are planning on changing your dog's menu, do so gradually to ensure that your dog will not have any problems. Over a period of four to five days, slowly add some new food to your dog's old food, increasing the percentage of new food each day.

INFORMATION...

Dog food must be at room temperature, neither too hot nor too cold. Fresh water, changed daily and served in a clean bowl, is mandatory, especially when feeding dried food.

Never feed your dog from the table while you are eating. Never feed your dog left-overs from your

own meal. They usually contain too much fat and too much seasoning.

Dogs must chew their food. Hard pellets are excellent; soups and slurries are to be avoided.

Don't add left-overs or any extras to normal dog food. The normal food is usually balanced and adding something extra destroys the balance.

Except for age-related changes, dogs do not require dietary variations. They can be fed the same diet, day after day, without their becoming ill.

GRAIN-BASED DIETS

Some less expensive dog foods are based on grains and other plant proteins. Whilst these products may appear to be attractively priced,

many breeders prefer a diet based on animal proteins and believe that they are more conducive to your dog's health. Many grain-based diets rely on soy protein that may cause flatulence (passing gas).

There are many cases, however, when your dog might require a special diet. These special requirements should only be recommended by your veterinary surgeon.

fit, it is essential to his mental well-being. A bored dog will find something to do, which often manifests itself in some type of destructive behaviour. In this sense, exercise is essential for the owner's mental well-being as well!

GROOMING

An important consideration of the breed is its coat. The baby puppy coat will be quite short, perhaps a little thick, but will be easily brushed and combed. When bathed, it won't take too long to dry. The parts that are white won't change colour, but the dense black parts seen at birth will eventually start to show signs of turning to blue-grey. Some, in time, will have a

DID YOU KNOW?

You should be careful where you exercise your dog. Many countryside areas have been sprayed with chemicals that are highly toxic to both dogs and humans. Never allow your dog to eat grass or drink from

puddles on either public or private grounds, as the run-off water may contain chemicals from sprays and herbicides.

dark charcoal grey shade, while others will be quite a deep blue. Sometimes you find a much paler silver-grey. The new adult coat will sometimes come through as silver, so pale as to appear little darker than the white parts. Eventually the deeper blue will grow in from the roots. While the coat is going through these changes of colour, it is said to be 'clearing.' If exhibited in a dog show, a knowledgeable judge will wish to know the age, so that allowance can be made for the coat's colour development. The texture will also alter with maturity.

The soft puppy coat will be replaced by a crisp and

GROOMING EQUIPMENT

How much grooming equipment you purchase will depend on how much grooming you are going to do. Here are some basics:
• Natural bristle brush
• Slicker brush
• Metal comb
• Scissors
• Blaster
• Rubber mat
• Dog shampoo
• Spray hose attachment
• Ear cleaner
• Cotton wipes
• Towels
• Nail clippers

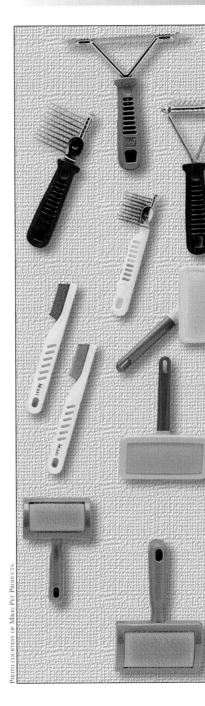

PHOTO COURTESY OF MIKKI PET PRODUCTS.

You will need to purchase grooming equipment to properly care for your Bobtail's coat. Your local pet shop should have a variety of items from which to choose.

Brushing an adult OES in full coat before a bath can be quite a chore.

undercoat can soon become matted (felted) and this causes unhealthy skin conditions. Additionally, 'visitors' in the form of fleas would soon find a comfortable place in which to live and multiply. If allowed to become totally out-of-control, then coats sometimes have to be clipped off.

BRUSHING

Begin training the puppy to stay calm for the brushing sessions. Use a grooming table, available from your local pet shop, to save time and the strain on your back. Even an adult dog can use the grooming table. As soon as the adolescent is big enough, you can train him to jump up. (Don't even think of picking him up to place him on the table.) Be sure the table has a non-slip mat to avoid the puppy becoming unruly while standing on the table. A natural bristle brush can be used for regular routine brushing, and a comb is handy to help remove mats. Brush the coat through thoroughly. Do not over-brush the Bobtail's coat as this can harm the coat by removing the undercoat.

Daily brushing is effective for removing dead hair and stimulating the dog's natural oils to add shine and a healthy look to the coat. Regular grooming sessions are also a

waterproof outer coat, followed by the growth of a softer undercoat. This 'double coat' is the insulated means to retain body heat in very cold weather, and the harsh outer hairs repel the rain, thus ensuring that the working dog will be comfortable in all weather conditions. As the weather turns warmer, there will be the natural discarding of the winter undercoat. If you are to keep your dog in a healthy and clean jacket, then regular time must be devoted to grooming. If left without attention, then the good way to spend time with your dog. Many dogs grow to like the feel of being brushed and will enjoy the daily routine.

BATHING

The Bobtail's coat care will necessarily include bathing as well. You can either find a local and trustworthy dog groomer or kennel that offers such a service, or undertake bathing yourself. If the family bathroom is to be used, then prepare it very carefully. Remove anything that might get knocked over or dampened by a shaking dog. It is very helpful if your bath has a shower hose attachment. We put about four inches of not too hot water in the bath, which ideally has either non-slipping strips on its bottom, or a firmly fixed rubber mat. Have ready all that your will need to use before attempting to take your dog in. Be sure that you have ample towels, shampoo, etc.

Before putting your dog in the bath, you will have ensured that teeth and ears are clean, and, if necessary, claws have been trimmed. Do check that there are no dew claws, which can easily be missed and may grow uncomfortably long. When both of you are in the bathroom, close the door very carefully—nobody wants a wet

dog running all over the house and furniture.

Place the dog carefully in the water, acting in a calm and reassuring manner. Either using the shower spray, or a plastic jug, wet the coat thoroughly before applying a good dog shampoo, which will normally be insecticidal. Work the shampoo carefully through the coat, taking care not to get it in the eyes. If you rub a Bobtail's coat too hard, you may cause it

The hair around the Bobtail's face is brushed out to give it a full, round look.

To make grooming the Bobtail a bit easier, an often-used method is to roll the dog on its side on the grooming table to brush out the coat.

GROOMING TIP

The use of human soap products like shampoo, bubble bath and hand soap can be damaging to a dog's coat and skin. Human products are too strong and remove the protective oils coating the dog's hair and skin (making him

water-resistant). Use only shampoo made especially for dogs and you may like to use a medicated shampoo, which will always help to keep external parasites at bay.

the front of the chest. Continue along the topline, down the sides of the body, making sure not to miss the area between the rib cage and the elbows.

GROOMING TIP

Once you are sure that the dog is thoroughly rinsed, squeeze the excess water out of the coat with your hand and dry him with a heavy towel. You may choose to use a blaster on his coat or just let it dry naturally. In cold weather, never allow your dog outside with a wet coat.

There are 'dry bath' products on the market, which are sprays and powders intended for spot cleaning, that can be used between regular baths, if necessary. They are not substitutes for regular baths, but they are easy to use for touch-ups as they do not require rinsing.

to mat-up in the undercoat. As the feet are usually the dirtiest parts, the soil will loosen while the dog stands in the water. Wash the feet thoroughly, they should shampoo and clean up quite well. When all the shampooing is done, then rinse carefully, starting at the highest part of the head, down the neck, under the chin and down

The long and short of it...
The sleek smooth coat of
the Dalmatian and the
abundant coat of the OES
are equally impressive
when well groomed, but
it's obvious which coat
requires more primping
to look its best.

Don't forget that there is also an under belly. When the body is rinsed off, then carry on to completion, and finish with the legs.

When completely rinsed, we always place towels over the dog to begin the drying process. We carefully blot out as much of the moisture as possible, before taking him from the bath. If you have any old candlewick bedspreads, they are quite excellent for absorbing water. Some folks may have access to a professional-type dog dryer, which tends to blast the water out of the coat. If that is not available, then you may resort to a hand-held dryer, but that will take considerably longer. Whatever method you use, it is essential that you don't let the dog loose until he is completely dry.

Canine natural reaction to having a good clean bath is to make for a most convenient spot, and have a good roll in something that is preferably smelly, very far from clean. If the dogs does need to go outdoors before he's dry, then take him out on a collar and lead, and bring him straight back indoors as soon as his toileting needs are met.

Should you decide to make use of outside help for bathing and grooming, do check that they will ensure teeth and ears are cleaned, claws are cut and any surplus hair from between the pads is trimmed out. Also, you must make it quite clear as to exactly how the coat is to be dealt with. We have all heard of owners leaving a fully coated dog for bathing and/or grooming, only to find on collection that its hair all has been clipped off. Professional dog grooming is not cheap, and it does involve several hours of labour, so do ascertain and agree upon the cost before making a booking. You get what you pay for, so it would be foolish to believe you'll get a complete service for little cost.

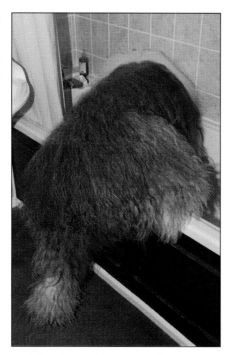

He knows the routine—this Bobtail is ready for his bath and he climbs into the tub all by himself! That's a well-trained dog.

EAR CLEANING

The ears should be kept clean and any excess hair inside the ear should be carefully plucked. Ears can be cleaned with a cotton wipe and ear powder made especially for dogs. Be on the lookout for any signs of infection or ear mite infestation. If your Bobtail has been shaking his head or scratching at his ears frequently, this usually indicates a problem. If his ears have an unusual odour, this is a sure sign of mite infestation or infection, and a signal to have his ears checked by the veterinary surgeon.

NAIL CLIPPING

Your Bobtail should be accustomed to having his nails trimmed at an early age, since it will be part of your mainte-nance routine throughout his life. Not only does it look nicer, but long nails can be sharp and scratch someone unintentionally. Also, a long nail has a better chance of ripping and bleeding, or causing the feet to spread. A good rule of thumb is that if you can hear your dog's nails clicking on the floor when he walks, his nails are too long.

Before you start cutting, make sure you can identify the 'quick' in each nail. The quick is a blood vessel that runs

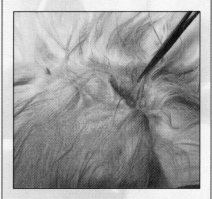

DID YOU KNOW?

Not every dog's ears are the same. Ears that are open to the air are healthier than ears with poor air circulation. Sometimes a dog can have two differently shaped ears. You should not probe inside your dog's ears. Only clean that which is accessible with a soft cotton wipe.

through the centre of each nail and grows rather close to the end. It will bleed if acciden-tally cut, which will be quite painful for the dog as it contains nerve endings. Keep some type of clotting agent on hand, such as a styptic pencil or styptic powder (the type used for shaving). This will stop the bleeding quickly when applied to the end of the cut nail. Do not panic if this happens, just stop the bleeding and talk soothingly to your dog. Once he has calmed down,

There are several types of nail clippers available that are designed especially for use on dogs.

Nail Maintenance

Nail Casing
Quick

Cut Line

Dark-Coloured Nails

With black or dark nails, where the quick is not easy to see, it's best to clip only the tip of the nail or to use a file.

Light-Coloured Nails

In light-coloured nails, clipping is much simpler because you can see the vein (or quick) that grows inside the casing.

move on to the next nail. It is better to clip a little at a time, particularly with black-nailed dogs.

Hold your pup steady as you begin trimming his nails; you do not want him to make any sudden movements or run away. Talk to him soothingly and stroke him as you clip. Holding his foot in your hand, simply take off the end of each nail in one quick clip. You can purchase nail clippers that are specially made for dogs; you can probably find them wherever you buy pet or grooming supplies.

The bottoms of your Bobtail's feet should be kept clean. The top photo shows an untrimmed paw. The lower photo shows the same paw after it has been properly trimmed.

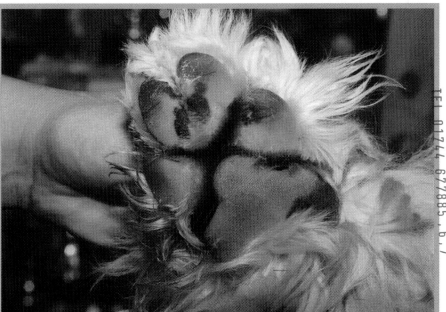

A dog that spends a lot of time outside on a hard surface, such as cement or pavement, will have his nails naturally worn down and may not need to have them trimmed as often, except maybe in the colder months when he is not outside as much. Regardless, it is best to get your dog accustomed to this

Never drive with your OES loose within the car. He should be secure in his crate if it fits in the car; another alternative is a dog safety harness that functions similarly to a seat belt.

procedure at an early age so that he is used to it. Some dogs are especially sensitive about having their feet touched, but if a dog has experienced it since he was young, he should not be bothered by it.

TRAVELLING WITH YOUR DOG

CAR TRAVEL

You should accustom your Bobtail to riding in a car at an early age. You may or may not take him in the car often, but at the very least he will need to go to the vet and you do not want these trips to be traumatic for the dog or problematic for you. The safest way for a dog to ride in the car is in his crate. If he uses a crate in the house, you can use the same crate for travel.

Put the pup in the crate and see how he reacts. If he seems uneasy, you can have a passenger hold him on his lap

while you drive. Another option is a specially made safety harness for dogs, which straps the dog in much like a seat belt. Do not let the dog roam loose in the vehicle—this is very dangerous! If you should stop short, your dog can be thrown and injured. If the dog starts climbing on you and pestering you while you are driving, you will not be able to concentrate on the road. It is an unsafe situation for everyone—human and canine.

For long trips, be prepared to stop to let the dog relieve himself. Bring along whatever you need to clean up after him. You should take along some paper kitchen towels and perhaps some old towelling for use should he have an accident in the car or suffer from travel sickness.

AIR TRAVEL

While it is possible to take a dog on a flight within Britain,

TRAVEL TIP

If you are going on a long motor trip with your dog, be sure the hotels are dog friendly. Many hotels do not accept dogs. Also take along some ice that can be thawed and offered to your dog if he becomes overheated. Most dogs like to lick ice.

FREE AT LAST!

Whilst running off lead may be great fun for your dog, it can turn into a time when your dog shows you everything you did wrong in obedience class. If you want to give your dog a chance to have some fun and exercise without the constraints of a leash, the best place to do this is

in a designated fenced-in area where dogs can socialise and work off excess energy. When visiting such an area, don't let your dog run amok or unattended, watch other dogs that are present, and follow all rules, specifically those regarding waste disposal.

MOTION SICKNESS

*If life is a motorway...*your dog may not want to come along for the ride! Some dogs experience motion sickness in cars that leads to excessive salivation and even vomiting. In most cases, your dog will fare better in the familiar, safe confines of his crate. To desensitise your dog, try going on

several short jaunts before trying a long trip. If your dog experiences distress when riding in the vehicle, drive with him only when absolutely necessary, and do not feed him or give him water before you go.

this is fairly unusual and advance permission is always required. The dog will be required to travel in a fibreglass crate and you should always check in advance with the airline regarding specific requirements. To help the dog be at ease, put one of his favourite toys in the crate with him. Do not feed the dog for at least six hours before the trip to minimise his need to relieve himself. However, certain regulations specify that water must always be made available to the dog in the crate.

Make sure your dog is properly identified and that your contact information appears on his ID tags and on his crate. Animals travel in a

TRAVEL TIP

For international travel you will have to make arrangements well in advance (perhaps months), as countries' regulations pertaining to bringing in animals differ. There may be special health certificates and/or vaccinations that your dog will need before taking the trip; sometimes this has to be done within a certain time frame. In rabies-free countries, you will need to bring proof of the dog's rabies vaccination and there may be a quarantine period upon arrival.

different area of the plane than human passengers so every rule must be strictly adhered to so as to prevent the risk of getting separated from your dog.

BOARDING

So you want to take a family holiday—and you want to include *all* members of the family. You would probably make arrangements for accommodation ahead of time anyway, but this is especially important when travelling with a dog. You do not want to make an overnight stop at the only place around for miles and find out that they do not allow dogs. Also, you do not want to reserve a place for your family without confirming that you are travelling with a dog because if it is against their policy you may not have a

TRAVEL TIP

The most extensive travel you do with your dog may be limited to trips to the veterinary surgeon's office—or you may decide to bring him along for long distances when the family goes on holiday. Whichever the case, it is important to consider your dog's safety while travelling.

place to stay.

Alternatively, if you are travelling and choose not to bring your Bobtail, you will have to make arrangements for him while you are away. Some options are to take him to a

ABUSING YOUR BEST FRIEND

As an educated and caring pet owner, you may believe that everyone wants to invest countless hours (and pounds) in order to raise a loving and well-adjusted canine companion. Sadly, this is not the case, as dogs account for almost half of all victims of animal abuse. Remember, abuse implies not only beating or torturing an animal but also neglecting the animal, such as failing to provide adequate shelter and food or emotional fulfilment.

CONSIDERATIONS ABOUT BOARDING

Will your dog be exercised at least twice a day? How much of the day will the staff keep him company? Does the kennel provide a clean and secure environment?
If the staff asks you a lot of questions, this is a good sign. They need to know your dog's personality and tempera-ment, health record, special require-ments, and what commands he has learned. Above all, follow your instincts. If you have a bad feeling about one kennel, even if a friend has recommended it, don't put your dog in their care.

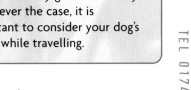

neighbour's house to stay while you are gone, to have a trusted neighbour pop in often or stay at your house, or bring your dog to a reputable boarding kennel. If you choose to board him at a kennel, you should visit in advance to see the facilities provided, how clean they are and where the dogs are kept. Talk to some of the employees and see how they treat the dogs—do they spend time with the dogs, play with them, exercise them, etc.? Also find out the kennel's policy on vaccinations and what they require. This is for all of the dogs' safety, since when dogs are kept together, there is a greater risk of diseases being passed from dog to dog.

DID YOU KNOW?

As puppies become more and more expensive, especially those puppies of high quality for showing and/or breeding, they have a greater chance of being stolen. The usual collar dog tag is, of course, easily removed. But there are two techniques that have become widely used for identification.

The puppy microchip implantation involves the injection of a small microchip, about the size of a corn kernel, under the skin of the dog. If your dog shows up at a clinic or shelter, or is offered for resale under less than savory circumstances, it can be positively identified by the microchip. The microchip is scanned and a registry quickly identifies you as the owner. This is not only protection against theft, but should the dog run away or go chasing a squirrel and get lost, you have a fair chance of getting it back.

Tattooing is done on various parts of the dog, from its belly to its cheeks. The number tattooed can be your telephone number or any other number which you can easily memorise. When professional dog thieves see a tattooed dog, they usually lose interest in it. Both microchipping and tattooing can be done at your local veterinary clinic. For the safety of our dogs, no laboratory facility or dog broker will accept a tattooed dog as stock.

When selecting a boarding kennel, be sure it has large enough runs to comfortably house an OES. Cleanliness, convenience and cost are the other considerations in selecting a suitable kennel for your dog.

IDENTIFICATION

If your dog gets lost, he is not able to ask for directions home.

Identification tags fastened to the collar give important information—the dog's name, the owner's name, the owner's address and a telephone number where the owner can be reached. This makes it easy for whom ever finds the dog to contact the owner and arrange to have the dog returned. An added advantage is that a person will be more likely to approach a lost dog who has ID tags on his collar; it tells the person that this is somebody's pet rather than a stray. This is the easiest and fastest method of identification provided that the tags stay on the collar and the collar stays on the dog.

IDENTIFICATION

Your Bobtail is your valued companion and friend. That is why you always keep a close eye on him and you have made sure that he cannot escape from the garden or wriggle out of his collar and run away from you. However, accidents can happen and there may come a time when your dog unexpectedly gets separated from you. If this unfortunate event should occur, the first thing on your mind will be finding him. Proper identification, including an ID tag, a tattoo, and possibly a microchip, will increase the chances of his being returned to you safely and quickly.

83

DID YOU KNOW?

If you start with a normal, healthy dog and give him time, patience and some carefully executed lessons, you will reap the rewards of that training for the life of the dog. And what a life it will be! The two of you will

find immeasurable pleasure in the companionship you have built together with love, respect and understanding.

Living with an untrained dog is a lot like owning a piano that you do not know how to play—it is a nice object to look at but it does not do much more than that to bring you pleasure. Now try taking piano lessons and suddenly the piano comes alive and brings forth magical sounds and rhythms that set your heart singing and your body swaying.

The same is true with your Bobtail. Any dog is a big responsibility and if not trained sensibly may develop unacceptable behaviour that annoys you or could even cause family friction.

To train your Bobtail, you may like to enrol in an obedience class. Teach him good manners as you learn how and why he behaves the way he does. Find out how to communicate with your dog and how to recognise and understand his communications with you. Suddenly the dog takes on a new role in your life—he is clever, interesting, well-behaved and fun to be with. He demonstrates his bond of devotion to you daily. In other words, your Bobtail does wonders for your ego because he constantly reminds you that you are not only his leader, you are his hero!

Those involved with teaching dog obedience and counselling owners about their dogs' behaviour have discovered some interesting facts about dog ownership. For example, training dogs when they are puppies results in the highest rate of success in developing well-mannered and well-adjusted adult dogs. Training an older dog, from six months to six years of age, can produce almost equal results providing that the owner accepts the dog's slower rate of learning capability and is willing to work patiently to help the dog succeed at developing to his fullest potential. Unfortunately, many owners of untrained adult dogs

TRAINING TIP

Training a dog is a life experience. Many parents admit that much of what they know about raising children they learned from caring for their dogs. Dogs respond to love, fairness and guidance, just as children do. Become a good dog owner and you may become an even better parent.

INFORMATION...

To a dog's way of thinking, your hands are like his mouth in terms of a defence mechanism. If you

squeeze him too tightly, he might just bite you because that would be his normal response. This is not aggressive biting and, although all biting should be discouraged, you need the discipline in learning how to handle your dog.

lack the patience factor, so they do not persist until their dogs are successful at learning

THINK BEFORE YOU BARK!

Dogs are sensitive to their master's moods and emotions. Use your voice wisely when communicating with your dog.

Never raise your voice at your dog unless you are angry and trying to correct him. 'Barking' at your dog can become as meaningless as 'dogspeak' is to you. Think before you bark!

The pup soaks up whatever you show him and constantly looks for more things to do and learn. At this early age, his body is not yet producing hormones, and therein lies the reason for such a high rate of success. Without hormones, he is focused on his owners and not particularly interested in investigating other places, dogs, people, etc. You are his leader: his provider of food, water, shelter and security. He latches onto you and wants to stay close. He will usually follow you from room to room, will not let you out of his sight when you are outdoors with him and will respond in like manner to the people and animals you encounter. If you greet a friend warmly, he will be happy to greet the person as well. If, however, you are hesitant, even anxious, about particular behaviours.

Training a puppy aged 10 to 16 weeks (20 weeks at the most) is like working with a dry sponge in a pool of water.

MEALTIME

Mealtime should be a peaceful time for your puppy. Do not put his food and water bowls in a high-traffic area in the house. For example, give him his own little corner of the kitchen where he can eat undisturbed and where he will not be under foot. Do not allow small children or other family members to disturb the pup when he is eating.

DID YOU KNOW?

Dogs are the most honourable animals in existence. They consider another species (humans) as their own. They interface with you. You are their leader. Puppies perceive children to be on their level; their actions around small children are different from their behaviour around their adult masters.

DID YOU KNOW?

Dogs will do anything for your attention. If you reward the dog when he is calm and resting, you will develop a well-mannered dog. If, on the other hand, you greet your dog excitedly and encourage him to

wrestle and roughhouse with you, the dog will greet you the same way and you will have a hyper dog on your hands.

the approach of a stranger, he will respond accordingly.

Once the puppy begins to produce hormones, his natural curiosity emerges and he begins to investigate the world around him. It is at this time when you may notice that the untrained dog begins to wander away from you and even ignore your commands to stay close. When this behaviour becomes a problem, the owner has two choices: get rid of the dog or train him. It is strongly urged that you choose the latter option.

There are usually classes within a reasonable distance from the owner's home, but you can also do a lot to train your dog yourself. Sometimes there are classes available but the tuition is too costly. Whatever the circumstances, the solution to the problem of lack of lesson availability lies within the pages of this book.

This chapter is devoted to helping you train your Bobtail at home. If the recommended procedures are followed faithfully, you may expect positive results that will prove rewarding both to you and your dog.

Whether your new charge is a puppy or a mature adult, the

TRAINING TIP

Your dog is actually training you at the same time you are training him. Dogs do things to get attention. They usually repeat whatever succeeds in getting your attention.

methods of teaching and the techniques we use in training basic behaviours are the same. After all, no dog, whether puppy or adult, likes harsh or inhumane methods. All creatures, however, respond favourably to gentle motivational methods and sincere praise and encouragement. Now let us get started.

HOUSEBREAKING
You can train a puppy to relieve itself wherever you choose, but this must be somewhere suitable. You should bear in mind from the outset that when your puppy is old enough to go out in public places, any canine deposits must be removed at once. You will always have to carry with you a small plastic bag or 'poop-scoop.'

Outdoor training includes such surfaces as grass, soil or earth and cement. Indoor training usually means training your dog to newspaper.

When deciding on the surface and location that you will want your Bobtail to use, be sure it is going to be permanent. Training your dog to grass and then changing your mind two months later is extremely difficult for both dog and owner.

Next, choose the command you will use each and every time you want your puppy to void. 'Be quick' and 'Hurry up' are examples of commands commonly used by dog owners.

Get in the habit of giving the puppy your chosen relief command before you take him out. That way, when he becomes an adult, you will be able to determine if he wants to go out when you ask him. A confirmation will be signs of interest, wagging his tail,

DID YOU KNOW?

Never line your pup's sleeping area with newspaper. Puppy litters are usually raised on newspaper and, once in your home, the puppy will immediately associate newspaper with voiding. Never put newspaper on any floor while housetraining, as this will only confuse the puppy. If you are paper-training him, use paper in his designated relief area ONLY. Finally, restrict water intake after evening meals. Offer a few licks at a time—never let a young puppy gulp water after meals.

Usually your male Bobtail will have a favourite tree, bush or the like upon which he relieves himself, thus marking his territory.

watching you intently, going to the door, etc.

PUPPY'S NEEDS

Puppy needs to relieve himself after play periods, after each meal, after he has been sleeping and any time he indicates that he is looking for a place to urinate or defecate.

The urinary and intestinal tract muscles of very young puppies are not fully developed. Therefore, like human babies, puppies need to relieve themselves frequently.

Take your puppy out often—every hour for an eight-week-old, for example, and always immediately after sleeping and eating. The older the puppy, the less often he will need to relieve himself. Finally, as a mature healthy adult, he will require only three to five relief trips per day.

89

CANINE DEVELOPMENT SCHEDULE

It is important to understand how and at what age a puppy develops into adulthood. If you are a puppy owner, consult the following Canine Development Schedule to determine the stage of development your puppy is currently experiencing. This knowledge will help you as you work with the puppy in the weeks and months ahead.

Period	Age	Characteristics
FIRST TO THIRD	**BIRTH TO SEVEN WEEKS**	Puppy needs food, sleep and warmth, and responds to simple and gentle touching. Needs mother for security and disciplining. Needs littermates for learning and interacting with other dogs. Pup learns to function within a pack and learns pack order of dominance. Begin socialising with adults and children for short periods. Begins to become aware of its environment.
FOURTH	**EIGHT TO TWELVE WEEKS**	Brain is fully developed. Needs socialising with outside world. Remove from mother and littermates. Needs to change from canine pack to human pack. Human dominance necessary. Fear period occurs between 8 and 16 weeks. Avoid fright and pain.
FIFTH	**THIRTEEN TO SIXTEEN WEEKS**	Training and formal obedience should begin. Less association with other dogs, more with people, places, situations. Period will pass easily if you remember this is pup's change-to-adolescence time. Be firm and fair. Flight instinct prominent. Permissiveness and over-disciplining can do permanent damage. Praise for good behaviour.
JUVENILE	**FOUR TO EIGHT MONTHS**	Another fear period about 7 to 8 months of age. It passes quickly, but be cautious of fright and pain. Sexual maturity reached. Dominant traits established. Dog should understand sit, down, come and stay by now.

NOTE: THESE ARE APPROXIMATE TIME FRAMES. ALLOW FOR INDIVIDUAL DIFFERENCES IN PUPPIES.

HOUSING

Since the types of housing and control you provide for your puppy have a direct relationship on the success of housetraining, we consider the various aspects of both before we begin training.

Bringing a new puppy home and turning him loose in your house can be compared to turning a child loose in a sports arena and telling the child that the place is all his! The sheer enormity of the place would be too much for him to handle.

Instead, offer the puppy clearly defined areas where he can play, sleep, eat and live. A room of the house where the family gathers is the most obvious choice. Puppies are social animals and need to feel a part of the pack right from the start. Hearing your voice, watching you whilst you are doing things and smelling you nearby are all positive reinforcers that he is now a member of your pack. Usually a family room, the kitchen or a

When you buy a crate of any kind, get one that is large enough to comfortably accommodate your OES when it is fully grown.

nearby adjoining breakfast area is ideal for providing safety and security for both puppy and owner.

Within that room there should be a smaller area which the puppy can call his own. An alcove, a wire or fibreglass dog crate or a fenced (not boarded!) corner from which he can view the activities of his new family will be fine. The size of the area or crate is the key factor here. The area must be large enough for the puppy to lie down and stretch out as well as stand up without rubbing his head on the top, yet small enough so that he cannot relieve himself at one end and

An open crate is fine for inside your home. For puppies, however, never put the water bowl inside the crate. This invites accidents when the puppy is crated.

91

sleep at the other without coming into contact with his droppings until fully trained to relieve himself outside.

Dogs are, by nature, clean animals and will not remain close to their relief areas unless forced to do so. In those cases, they then become dirty dogs and usually remain that way for life.

The designated area should be lined with clean bedding and a toy. Water must always be available, in a non-spill container.

THE GOLDEN RULE

The golden rule of dog training is simple. For each 'question' (command), there is only one correct answer (reaction). One command = one reaction. Keep practising the command until the dog reacts

correctly without hesitating. Be repetitive but not monotonous. Dogs get bored just as people do!

CONTROL

By control, we mean helping the puppy to create a lifestyle pattern that will be compatible to that of his human pack (YOU!). Just as we guide little children to learn our way of life, we must show the puppy when it is time to play, eat, sleep, exercise and even entertain himself.

Your puppy should always sleep in his crate. He should also learn that, during times of household confusion and excessive human activity such as at breakfast when family members are preparing for the day, he can play by himself in relative safety and comfort in his designated area. Each time you leave the puppy alone, he should understand exactly where he is to stay. Puppies are chewers. They cannot tell the difference between lamp cords, television wires, shoes, table legs, etc. Chewing into a television wire, for example, can be fatal to the puppy whilst a shorted wire can start a fire in the house.

If the puppy chews the arm of the chair when he is alone, you will probably discipline him angrily when you get home. Thus, he makes the association that your coming home means he is going to be punished. (He will not remember chewing the chair and is incapable of making the association of the discipline with his naughty deed.)

Other times of excitement, such as family parties, etc., can be fun for the puppy providing he can view the activities from the security of his designated area. He is not underfoot and he is not being fed all sorts of titbits that will probably cause him stomach distress, yet he still feels a part of the fun.

SCHEDULE

A puppy should be taken to his relief area each time he is released from his designated area, after meals, after a play session and when he first awakens in the morning (at age eight weeks, this can mean 5 a.m.!). The puppy will indicate that he's ready 'to go' by circling or sniffing busily—do not misinterpret these signs. For a puppy less than ten weeks of age, a routine of taking him out every hour is necessary. As the puppy grows, he will be able to wait for longer periods of time.

Keep trips to his relief area short. Stay no more than five or six minutes and then return to the house. If he goes during that time, praise him lavishly and take him indoors immediately. If he does not, but he has an accident when you go back indoors, pick him up immedi-

PRACTICE MAKES PERFECT!

• Have training lessons with your dog every day in several short segments—three to five times a day for a few minutes at a time is ideal.
• Do not have long practice sessions. The dog will become easily bored.

• Never practise when you are tired, ill, worried or in an otherwise negative mood. This will transmit to the dog and may have an adverse effect on its performance.

Think fun, short and above all POSITIVE! End each session on a high note, rather than a failed exercise, and make sure to give a lot of praise. Enjoy the training and help your dog enjoy it, too.

ately, say 'No! No!' and return to his relief area. Wait a few minutes, then return to the house again. Never hit a puppy

HOW MANY TIMES A DAY?

AGE	RELIEF TRIPS
To 14 weeks	10
14–22 weeks	8
22–32 weeks	6
Adulthood	4
(dog stops growing)	

These are estimates, of course, but they are a guide to the MINIMUM opportunities a dog should have each day to relieve itself.

or rub his face in urine or excrement when he has had an accident!

Once indoors, put the puppy in his crate until you have had time to clean up his accident. Then release him to the family area and watch him more closely than before. Chances are, his accident was a result of your not picking up his signal or waiting too long before offering him the opportunity to relieve himself. Never hold a grudge against the

THE SUCCESS METHOD

1 Tell the puppy 'Crate time!' and place him in the crate with a small treat (a piece of cheese or half of a biscuit). Let him stay in the crate for five minutes while you are in the same room. Then release him and praise lavishly. Never release him when he is fussing. Wait until he is quiet before you let him out.

2 Repeat Step 1 several times a day.

3 The next day, place the puppy in the crate as before. Let him stay there for ten minutes. Do this several times.

4 Continue building time in five-minute increments until the puppy

stays in his crate for 30 minutes with you in the room. Always take him to his relief area after prolonged periods in his crate.

5 Now go back to Step 1 and let the puppy stay in his crate for five minutes, this time while you are out of the room.

6 Once again, build crate time in five-minute increments with you out of the room. When the puppy will stay willingly in his crate (he may even fall asleep!) for 30 minutes with you out of the room, he will be ready to stay in it for several hours at a time.

6 Steps to Successful Crate Training

puppy for accidents.

Let the puppy learn that going outdoors means it is time to relieve himself, not play. Once trained, he will be able to play indoors and out and still differentiate between the times for play versus the times for relief.

Help him develop regular hours for naps, being alone, playing by himself and just resting, all in his crate. Encourage him to entertain himself whilst you are busy with your activities. Let him learn that having you near is comforting, but it is not your main purpose in life to provide him with undivided attention.

Each time you put a puppy in his own area, use the same command, whatever suits best. Soon he will run to his crate or special area when he hears you say those words.

THE SUCCESS METHOD

Success that comes by luck is usually short lived. Success that comes by well-thought-out proven methods is often more easily achieved and permanent. This is the Success Method. It is designed to give you, the puppy owner, a simple yet proven way to help your puppy develop clean living habits and a feeling of security in his new environment.

TRAINING TIP

Stand up straight and authoritatively when giving your dog commands. Do not issue commands when lying on the floor or lying on your back on

the sofa. If you are on your hands and knees when you give a command, your dog will think you are positioning yourself to play.

Crate training provides safety for you, the puppy and the home. It also provides the puppy with a feeling of security, and that helps the puppy achieve self-confidence and clean habits.

Remember that one of the primary ingredients in housetraining your puppy is control. Regardless of your lifestyle, there will always be occasions when you will need to have a place where your dog can stay and be happy and safe. Crate training is the answer for now and in the future.

Always clean up after your dog, whether you're in a public place or your own garden.

In conclusion, a few key elements are really all you need for a successful house training method—consistency, frequency, praise, control and supervision. By following these

DID YOU KNOW?

By providing sleeping and resting quarters that fit the dog, and offering frequent opportunities to relieve himself outside his quarters, the puppy quickly learns that the outdoors (or the newspaper if you are training him to paper) is the place to go when he needs to urinate or defecate. It also reinforces his innate desire to keep his sleeping quarters clean. This, in turn, helps develop the muscle control that will eventually produce a dog with clean living habits.

HOUSEBREAKING TIP

Do not carry your dog to his toilet area. Lead him there on a leash or, better yet, encourage him to follow

you to the spot. If you start carrying him to his spot, you might end up doing this routine forever and your dog will have the satisfaction of having trained YOU.

procedures with a normal, healthy puppy, you and the puppy will soon be past the stage of 'accidents' and ready to move on to a full and rewarding life together.

ROLES OF DISCIPLINE, REWARD AND PUNISHMENT

Discipline, training one to act in accordance with rules, brings order to life. It is as simple as that. Without discipline, particularly in a group society, chaos reigns supreme and the group will eventually perish. Humans and canines are social animals and need some form of discipline in order to function effectively. They must procure food, protect their home base and their young and reproduce to keep the species going.

If there were no discipline in the lives of social animals, they would eventually die from starvation and/or predation by other stronger animals.

In the case of domestic canines, dogs need discipline in their lives in order to understand how their pack (you and other family members) functions and how they must act in order to survive.

A large humane society in a highly populated area recently surveyed dog owners regarding their satisfaction with their relationships with their dogs. People who had trained their dogs were 75% more satisfied with their pets than those who had never trained their dogs.

Dr Edward Thorndike, a psychologist, established *Thorndike's Theory of Learning*, which states that a behaviour that results in a

DID YOU KNOW?

If you want to be successful in training your dog, you have four rules to obey yourself:
1. Develop an understanding of how a dog thinks.

2. Do not blame the dog for lack of communication.
3. Define your dog's personality and act accordingly.
4. Have patience and be consistent.

TRAINING TIP

Never train your dog, puppy or adult, when you are angry or in a sour mood. Dogs are very sensitive to human feelings, especially anger, and if your dog senses that you are angry or upset, he will connect your anger with his training and learn to resent or fear his training sessions.

pleasant event tends to be repeated. A behaviour that results in an unpleasant event tends not to be repeated. It is this theory on which training methods are based today. For example, if you manipulate a dog to perform a specific behaviour and reward him for doing it, he is likely to do it again because he enjoyed the end result.

Exercise for a very young puppy can consist of a short walk around the house or garden. Playing can include fetching games with a large ball or a special raggy. (All puppies teethe and need soft things upon which to chew.) Remember to restrict play periods to indoors within his living area (the family room, for example) until he is completely housetrained.

Occasionally, punishment, a penalty inflicted for an offence, is necessary. The best type of punishment often comes from an outside source. For example, a child is told not to touch the stove because he may get burned. He disobeys and touches the stove. In doing so, he receives a burn. From that time on, he respects the heat of the stove and avoids contact with it. Therefore, a behaviour that results in an unpleasant event tends not to be repeated.

A good example of a dog learning the hard way is the dog who chases the house cat. He is told many times to leave the cat alone, yet he persists in teasing the cat. Then, one day he begins chasing the cat but the cat turns and swipes a claw across the dog's face, leaving him with a painful gash on his nose. The final result is that the dog stops chasing the cat.

TRAINING EQUIPMENT

COLLAR AND LEAD
For a Bobtail the collar and lead that you use for training must be one with which you are easily able to work, not too heavy for the dog and perfectly safe.

TREATS
Have a bag of treats on hand. Something nutritious and easy

If you have other pets in the home and/or interact often with the pets of friends and other family members, your pup will respond to those pets in much the same manner as you do. It is only when you show fear of or resentment toward another animal that he will act fearful or unfriendly.

HOUSEBREAKING TIP

Most of all, be consistent. Always take your dog to the same location, always use the same command, and always have him on lead when he is in his relief area, unless a fenced-in garden is available.

to swallow works best. Use a soft treat, a chunk of cheese or a piece of cooked chicken rather than a dry biscuit. By the time the dog has finished chewing a dry treat, he will forget why he is being rewarded in the first place! Using food rewards will not teach a dog to beg at the table— the only way to teach a dog to beg at the table is to give him food from the table. In training, rewarding the dog with a food treat will help him associate praise and the treats with learning new behaviours that obviously please his owner.

DID YOU KNOW?

Dogs are as different from each other as people are. What works for one dog may not work for another. Have an open mind. If one method of training is unsuccessful, try another.

By following the Success Method, your puppy will be completely housetrained by the time his muscle and brain development reach maturity. Keep in mind that small breeds usually mature faster than large breeds, but all puppies should be trained by six months of age.

What a motivator food can be! Soft cheese, small bits of chicken or freeze-dried liver are all healthful and tasty treats.

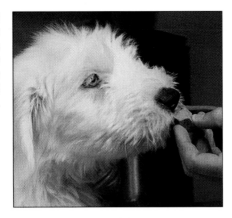

TRAINING BEGINS: ASK THE DOG A QUESTION

In order to teach your dog anything, you must first get his attention. After all, he cannot learn anything if he is looking away from you with his mind on something else.

To get his attention, ask him, 'School?' and immediately walk over to him and give him a treat as you tell him 'Good dog.' Wait a minute or two and repeat the routine, this time with a treat in your hand as you approach within a foot of the dog. Do not go directly to him, but stop about a foot short of him and hold out the treat as you ask, 'School?' He will see you approaching with a treat in your hand and most likely begin walking toward you. As you meet, give him the treat and praise again.

The third time, ask the question, have a treat in your hand and walk only a short distance toward the dog so that he must walk almost all the way to you. As he reaches you, give him the treat and praise again.

By this time, the dog will probably be getting the idea that if he pays attention to you, especially when you ask that question, it will pay off in treats and enjoyable activities for him. In other words, he learns that 'school' means doing enjoyable things with you that result in treats and positive attention for him.

THE STUDENT'S STRESS TEST

During training sessions you must be able to recognise signs of stress in your dog such as:
- tucking his tail between his legs
- lowering his head
- shivering or trembling
- standing completely still or running away
- panting and/or salivating
- avoiding eye contact
- flattening his ears back
- urinating submissively
- rolling over and lifting a leg
- grinning or baring teeth
- aggression when restrained

If your four-legged student displays these signs he may just be nervous or intimidated. The training session may have been too lengthy with not enough praise and affirmation. Stop for the day and try again tomorrow.

Remember that the dog does not understand your verbal language; he only recognises sounds. Your question translates to a series of sounds for him, and those sounds become the signal to go to you and pay attention; if he does, he will get to interact with you plus receive treats and praise.

THE BASIC COMMANDS

TEACHING SIT

Now that you have the dog's attention, attach his lead and hold it in your left hand and a food treat in your right. Place

SAFETY FIRST

Whilst it may seem that the most important things to your dog are eating, sleeping and chewing the upholstery on your furniture, his first concern is actually safety. The domesticated dogs we keep as companions have the same pack instinct as their ancestors who ran free thousands of years ago. Because of this pack instinct, your dog wants to know that he and his pack are not in danger of being harmed, and that his pack has a strong, capable leader. You must establish yourself as the leader early on in your relationship. That way your dog will trust that you will take care of him and the pack, and he will accept your commands without question.

FEAR AGGRESSION

Pups who are subjected to physical abuse during training commonly end up with behavioural problems as adults. One common result of abuse is fear aggression, in which a dog will lash out, bare his teeth, snarl and finally bite someone by whom he feels threatened. For example, your daughter may be playing with the dog one afternoon. As they play hide-and-seek, she backs the dog into a corner, and as she attempts to tease him playfully, he bites her hand. Examine the cause of this behaviour. Did your daughter ever hit the dog? Did someone who resembles your daughter hit or scream at the dog? Fortunately, fear aggression is relatively easy to correct. Have your daughter engage in only positive activities with the dog, such as feeding, petting and walking. She should not give any corrections or negative feedback. If the dog still growls or cowers away from her, allow someone else to accompany them. After approximately one week, the dog should feel that he can rely on her for many positive things, and he will also be prevented from reacting fearfully towards anyone who might resemble her.

SIT is a basic exercise and one of the easiest to teach. It just takes patience and persistence.

your food hand at the dog's nose and let him lick the treat but not take it from you. Say 'Sit' and slowly raise your food hand from in front of the dog's nose up over his head so that he is looking at the ceiling. As he bends his head upward, he will have to bend his knees to maintain his balance. As he bends his knees, he will assume a sit position. At that point, release the food treat and praise lavishly with comments such as 'Good dog! Good sit!,' etc. Remember to always praise enthusiastically, because dogs relish verbal praise from their owners and feel so proud of themselves whenever they accomplish a behaviour.

You will not use food

TRAINING TIP

Dogs do not understand our language. They can be trained to react to a certain sound, at a certain volume. If you say 'No, Oliver' in a very soft pleasant voice it will not have the same meaning as 'No, Oliver!!' when you shout it as loud as you can. You should never use the dog's name during a reprimand, just the command NO!! Since dogs don't understand words, comics often use dogs trained with opposite meanings. Thus, when the comic commands his dog to SIT the dog will stand up, and vice versa.

forever in getting the dog to obey your commands. Food is only used to teach new behaviours, and once the dog knows what you want when you give a specific command, you will wean him off the food treats but still maintain the verbal praise. After all, you will always have your voice with you, and there will be many times when you have no food rewards but expect the dog to obey.

TEACHING DOWN

Teaching the down exercise is easy when you understand how the dog perceives the down position, and it is very difficult when you do not. Dogs perceive the down position as a submissive one, therefore teaching the down exercise using a forceful method can sometimes make the dog develop such a fear of the down that he either runs away when you say 'Down' or he attempts to snap at the person who tries to force him down.

Have the dog sit close alongside your left leg, facing in the same direction as you are. Hold the lead in your left hand and a food treat in your right. Now place your left hand lightly on the top of the dog's shoulders where they meet above the spinal cord. Do not push down on the dog's

SAFETY FIRST

Whilst it may seem that the most important things to your dog are eating, sleeping and chewing the upholstery on your furniture, his first concern is actually safety. The domesticated dogs we keep as companions have the same pack instinct as their ancestors who ran

free thousands of years ago. Because of this pack instinct, your dog wants to know that he and his pack are not in danger of being harmed, and that his pack has a strong, capable leader. You must establish yourself as the leader early on in your relationship. That way your dog will trust that you will take care of him and the pack, and he will accept your commands without question.

shoulders; simply rest your left hand there so you can guide the dog to lie down close to your left leg rather than to swing away from your side

CONSISTENCY PAYS OFF

Dogs need consistency in their feeding schedule, exercise and toilet breaks and in the verbal commands you use. If you use 'Stay' on Monday and 'Stay here, please' on Tuesday, you will confuse your dog. Don't demand perfect behaviour during training classes and then let him have the run of the house the rest of the day. Above all, lavish praise on your pet consistently every time he does something right. The more he feels he is pleasing you, the more willing he will be to learn.

when he drops.

Now place the food hand at the dog's nose, say 'Down' very softly (almost a whisper), and slowly lower the food hand to the dog's front feet. When the food hand reaches the floor, begin moving it forward along the floor in front of the dog. Keep talking softly to the dog, saying things like, 'Do you want this treat? You can do this, good dog.' Your reassuring tone of voice will help calm the dog as he tries to follow the food hand in order to get the treat.

When the dog's elbows touch the floor, release the food and praise softly. Try to get the dog to maintain that down position for several seconds before you let him sit up again.

The goal here is to get the dog to settle down and not feel threatened in the down position.

TEACHING STAY

It is easy to teach the dog to stay in either a sit or a down position. Again, we use food and praise during the teaching process as we help the dog to understand exactly what it is that we are expecting him to do.

To teach the sit/stay, start with the dog sitting on your left side as before and hold the lead in your left hand. Have a food treat in your right hand and place your food hand at the dog's nose. Say 'Stay' and step out on your right foot to stand directly in front of the dog, toe

DID YOU KNOW?

Occasionally, a dog and owner who have not attended formal classes have been able to earn entry-level titles by obtaining competition rules and regulations from a local kennel club and practising on their own to a degree of perfection. Obtaining the higher level titles, however, almost always requires extensive training under the tutelage of experienced instructors. In addition, the more difficult levels require more specialised equipment whereas the lower levels do not.

Pups will be pups! There will be times when your puppy misbehaves or when it seems like his mind is on something other than the lesson at hand. Your patience will pay off, though, and the time you put in to teach your OES puppy will reward you with a well-behaved pet and companion.

HOW TO WEAN THE 'TREAT HOG'

If you have trained your dog by rewarding him with a treat each time he performs a command, he may soon decide that without the treat, he won't sit, stay or come. The best

way to fix this problem is to start asking your dog to do certain commands twice before being rewarded. Slowly increase the number of commands given and then vary the number: three sits and a treat one day, five sits for a biscuit the next day. Your dog will soon realise that there is no set number of sits before he gets his reward, and he'll likely do it the first time you ask in the hope of being rewarded sooner rather than later.

to toe, as he licks and nibbles the treat. Be sure to keep his head facing upward to maintain the sit position. Count to five and then swing around to stand next to the dog again with him on your left. As soon as you get back to the original position, release the food and praise lavishly.

To teach the down/stay, do the down as previously described. As soon as the dog lies down, say 'Stay' and step out on your right foot just as you did in the sit/stay. Count to five and then return to stand beside the dog with him on your left side. Release the treat and praise as always.

Within a week or ten days, you can begin to add a bit of distance between you and your dog when you leave him. When you do, use your left hand open with the palm facing the dog as a stay signal, much the same as the hand signal a constable uses to stop traffic at an intersection. Hold the food treat in your right hand as before, but this time the food is not touching the dog's nose. He will watch the food hand and quickly learn that he is going to get that treat as soon as you return to his side.

When you can stand 1 metre away from your dog for 30 seconds, you can then begin building time and distance in both stays. Eventually, the dog can be expected to remain in the stay position for prolonged periods of time until you return to him or call him to you. Always praise lavishly when he stays.

TEACHING COME

If you make teaching 'come' an enjoyable experience, you should never have a 'student' that does not love the game or that fails to come when called. The secret, it seems, is never to teach the word 'come.'

At times when an owner most wants his dog to come when called, the owner is likely upset or anxious and he allows these feelings to come through in the tone of his voice when he calls his dog. Hearing that desperation in his owner's voice, the dog fears the results of going to him and therefore either disobeys outright or runs in the opposite direction. The

TRAINING TIP

When calling the dog, do not say 'Come.' Say things like, 'Rover, where are you? See if you can find me! I have a biscuit for you!' Keep up a constant line of chatter with coaxing sounds and frequent questions such as, 'Where are you?' The dog will learn to follow the sound of your voice to locate you and receive his reward.

TRAINING TIP

Never call your dog to come to you for a correction or scold him when he reaches you. That is the quickest way to turn a 'Come' command into 'Go away fast!' Dogs think only in the present tense, and your dog will connect the scolding with coming to you, not with the misbehaviour of a few moments earlier.

secret, therefore, is to teach the dog a game and, when you want him to come to you, simply play the game. It is practically a no-fail solution!

To begin, have several members of your family take a few food treats and each go into a different room in the house. Take turns calling the dog, and each person should celebrate the dog's finding him with a treat and lots of happy praise. When a person calls the dog, he is actually inviting the dog to find him and get a treat as a reward for 'winning.'

A few turns of the 'Where are you?' game and the dog will understand that everyone is playing the game and that each person has a big celebration awaiting his success at locating him. Once he learns to love the game, simply calling out 'Where are you?' will bring him running from wherever he is when he hears that all-important question.

The come command is recognised as one of the most important things to teach a dog, but there are trainers who work with thousands of dogs and never teach the actual word 'come.' Yet these dogs will race to respond to a person who uses the dog's name followed by 'Where are you?' For example, a woman has a 12-year-old companion dog who went blind, but who never fails to locate her owner when asked, 'Where are you?'

Children, in particular, love to play this game with their dogs. Children can hide in smaller places like a shower or bath, behind a bed or under a table. The dog needs to work a little bit harder to find these hiding places, but when he does he loves to celebrate with a treat and a tussle with a favourite youngster.

> ### TRAINING TIP
>
> Teach your dog to HEEL in an enclosed area. Once you think the dog will obey reliably and you want to attempt advanced obedience exercises such as off-lead heeling, test him in a fenced-in area so he cannot run away.

TEACHING HEEL

Heeling means that the dog walks beside the owner without pulling. It takes time and patience on the owner's part to succeed at teaching the dog that he (the owner) will not proceed unless the dog is walking calmly beside him. Pulling out ahead on the lead is definitely not acceptable.

Begin by holding the lead in your left hand as the dog sits beside your left leg. Move the loop end of the lead to your right hand but keep your left hand short on the lead so it keeps the dog in close next to you.

Say 'Heel' and step forward on your left foot. Keep the dog close to you and take three steps. Stop and have the dog sit next to you in what we now call the 'heel position.' Praise verbally, but do not touch the dog. Hesitate a moment and begin again with 'Heel,' taking three steps and stopping, at which point the dog is told to sit again.

Your goal here is to have the dog walk those three steps without pulling on the lead. When he will walk calmly beside you for three steps without pulling, increase the number of steps you take to five. When he will walk politely beside you whilst you take five steps, you can increase the length of your walk to ten steps. Keep increasing the length of your stroll until the dog will walk quietly beside you without pulling as long as you want him to heel. When you stop heeling, indicate to the dog that the exercise is over by verbally praising as you pet him and say 'OK, good dog.' The 'OK' is used as a release word meaning that the exercise is finished and the dog is free to relax.

If you are dealing with a dog who insists on pulling you around, simply 'put on your brakes' and stand your ground until the dog realises that the two of you are not going anywhere until he is beside you

---

TRAINING TIP

If you begin teaching the heel by taking long walks and letting the dog pull you along, he misinterprets this action as an acceptable form of

taking a walk. When you pull back on the lead to counteract his pulling, he reads that tug as a signal to pull even harder!

TRAINING TIP

If you are walking your dog and he suddenly stops and looks straight into your eyes, ignore him. Pull the leash and lead him into the direction you want to walk.

---

and moving at your pace, not his. It may take some time just standing there to convince the dog that you are the leader and you will be the one to decide on the direction and speed of your travel.

Each time the dog looks up at you or slows down to give a slack lead between the two of

OBEDIENCE SCHOOL

A basic obedience beginner's class usually lasts for six to eight weeks. Dog and owner attend an hour-long lesson once a week and practise for a few minutes, several times a day, each day at home. If done properly, the whole procedure will result in a well-mannered dog and an owner who delights in living with a pet that is eager to please and enjoys doing things with his owner.

you, quietly praise him and say, 'Good heel. Good dog.' Eventually, the dog will begin to respond and within a few days he will be walking politely beside you without pulling on the lead. At first, the training sessions should be kept short and very positive; soon the dog will be able to walk nicely with you for increasingly longer distances. Remember also to give the dog free time and the opportunity to run and play when you have finished heel practice.

WEANING OFF FOOD IN TRAINING

Food is used in training new behaviours. Once the dog understands what behaviour goes with a specific command, it is time to start weaning him off the food treats. At first, give a treat after each exercise.

Then, start to give a treat only after every other exercise. Mix up the times when you offer a food reward and the times when you only offer praise so that the dog will never know when he is going to receive both food and praise and when he is going to receive only praise. This is called a variable ratio reward system and it proves successful because there is always the chance that the owner will produce a treat, so the dog never stops trying for that reward. No matter what, ALWAYS give verbal praise.

OBEDIENCE CLASSES

It is a good idea to enrol in an obedience class if one is available in your area. If yours is a show dog, ringcraft classes would be more appropriate. Many areas have dog clubs that offer basic obedience training as well as preparatory classes for obedience competition. There are also local dog trainers who offer similar classes.

At obedience trials, dogs can earn titles at various levels of competition. The beginning levels of competition include basic behaviours such as sit, down, heel, etc. The more advanced levels of competition include jumping, retrieving, scent discrimination and signal work. The advanced levels require a dog and owner to put a lot of time and effort into their training and the titles that can be earned at these levels of competition are very prestigious.

OTHER ACTIVITIES FOR LIFE

Whether a dog is trained in the structured environment of a class or alone with his owner at home, there are many activities that can bring fun and rewards to both owner and dog once they have mastered basic control.

Teaching the dog to help out around the home, in the garden or on the farm provides great satisfaction to both dog and owner. In addition, the dog's help makes life a little easier for his owner and raises his stature as a valued companion to his family. It helps give the dog a purpose by occupying his mind and providing an outlet for his energy.

Backpacking is an exciting and healthy activity that the dog can be taught without assistance from more than his owner. The exercise of walking and climbing is good for man and dog alike, and the bond that they develop together is priceless.

If you are interested in participating in organised competition with your Bobtail,

there are activities other than obedience in which you and your dog can become involved. Agility is a popular and enjoyable sport where dogs run through an obstacle course that includes various jumps, tunnels and other exercises to test the dog's speed and coordination. The owners run beside their dogs to give commands and to guide them through the course. Although competitive, the focus is on fun—it's fun to do, fun to watch and great exercise.

Every dog, whether pet or show, should be trained to walk politely on lead. The HEEL command is used in the show ring as the judges evaluate each dog's gait.

111

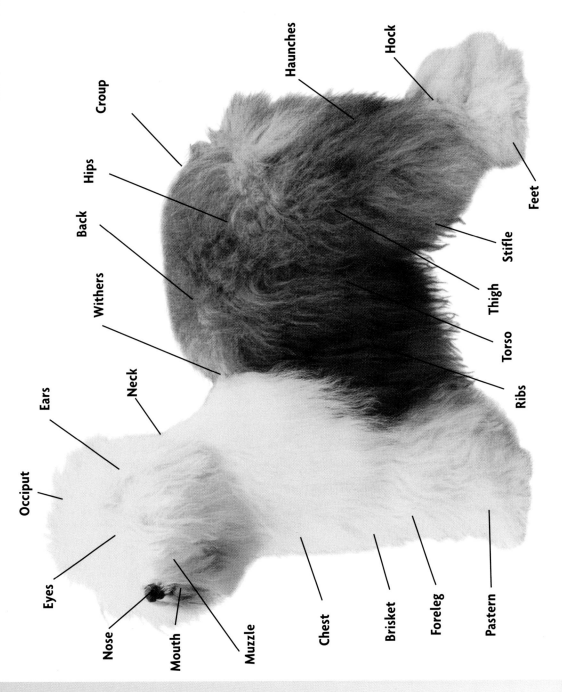

Physical Structure of the Old English Sheepdog

Dogs suffer many of the same physical illnesses as people. They might even share many of the same psychological problems. Since people usually know more about human diseases than canine maladies, many of the terms used in this chapter will be familiar but not necessarily those used by veterinary surgeons. We will use the term *x-ray*, instead of the more acceptable term *radiograph*. We will also use the familiar term *symptoms* even though dogs don't have symptoms, which are verbal descriptions of the patient's feelings; dogs have *clinical signs*. Since dogs can't speak, we have to look for clinical signs...but we still use the term *symptoms* in this book.

As a general rule, medicine is *practised*. That term is not arbitrary. Medicine is a constantly changing art as we learn more and more about genetics, electronic aids (like CAT scans) and daily laboratory advances. There are many dog maladies, like canine hip dysplasia, which are not universally treated in the same manner. Some veterinary surgeons opt for surgery more often than others do.

SELECTING A VETERINARY SURGEON

Your selection of a veterinary surgeon should not be based upon personality (as most are) but upon their convenience to your home. You require a veterinary surgeon who is close because you might have emergencies or need to make multiple visits for treatments. You require a vet who has services that you might require such as tattooing and grooming, as well as sophisticated pet supplies and a good reputation for ability and responsiveness. There is nothing more frustrating than having to wait a day or more to get a response from your veterinary surgeon.

Before you buy a dog, meet and interview the veterinary surgeons in your area. Take everything into consideration; discuss background, specialities, fees, emergency policies, etc.

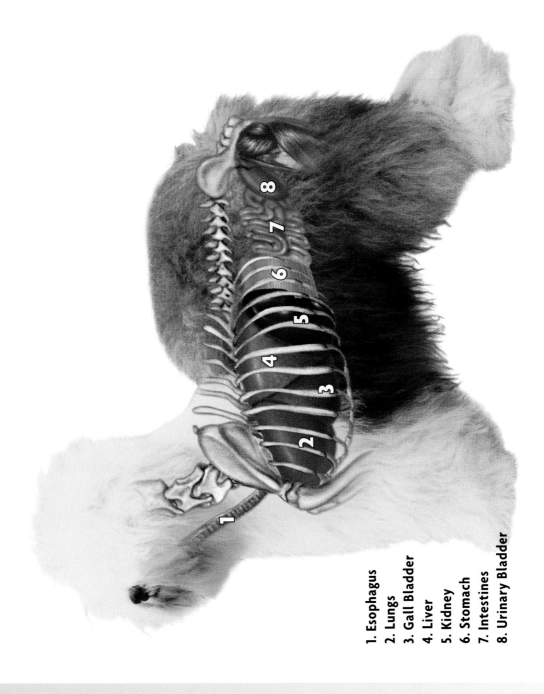

1. Esophagus
2. Lungs
3. Gall Bladder
4. Liver
5. Kidney
6. Stomach
7. Intestines
8. Urinary Bladder

Internal Organs of the Old English Sheepdog

All veterinary surgeons are licensed and their diplomas and/or certificates should be displayed in their waiting rooms. There are, however, many veterinary specialities that usually require further studies and internships. There are specialists in heart problems (veterinary cardiologists), skin problems (veterinary dermatologists), teeth and gum problems (veterinary dentists), eye problems (veterinary ophthalmologists) and x-rays (veterinary radiologists), and surgeons who have specialities in bones, muscles or other organs. Most veterinary surgeons do routine surgery such as neutering, stitching up wounds and docking tails for those breeds in which such is required for show purposes. When the problem affecting your dog is serious, it is not unusual or impudent to get another medical opinion, although in Britain you are obliged to advise the vets concerned about this. You might also want to compare costs

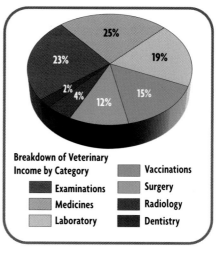

Breakdown of Veterinary Income by Category

- Examinations
- Medicines
- Laboratory
- Vaccinations
- Surgery
- Radiology
- Dentistry

A typical American vet's income, categorised according to services provided. This survey dealt with small-animal practices.

amongst several veterinary surgeons. Sophisticated health care and veterinary services can be very costly. Important decisions are often based upon financial considerations.

PREVENTATIVE MEDICINE
It is much easier, less costly and more effective to practise preventative medicine than to fight bouts of illness and disease. Properly bred puppies come from parents that were selected based upon their genetic disease profile. Their mothers should have been vaccinated, free of all internal and external parasites, and properly nourished. For these reasons, a visit to the veterinary surgeon who cared for the dam is recommended. The dam can pass on disease resistance to her puppies, which can last for eight to ten weeks. She can also pass on

DID YOU KNOW?

Male dogs are neutered. The operation removes the testicles and requires that the dog be anaesthetised. Recovery takes about one week. Females are spayed. This is major surgery and it usually takes a bitch two weeks to recover.

115

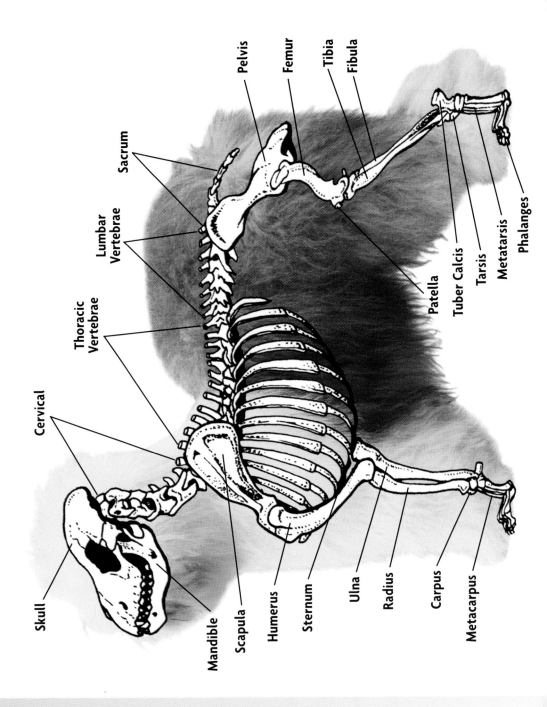

Skeletal Structure of the Old English Sheepdog

parasites and many infections. That's why you should visit the veterinary surgeon who cared for the dam.

VACCINATION SCHEDULING
Most vaccinations are given by injection and should only be done by a veterinary surgeon. Both he and you should keep a record of the date of the injection, the identification of the vaccine and the amount given. Some vets give a first vaccination at eight weeks, but most dog breeders prefer the course not to commence until about ten weeks because of negating any antibodies passed on by the dam. The vaccination scheduling is usually based on a 15-day cycle. You must take your vet's advice as to when to vaccinate as this may differ according to the vaccine used. Most vaccinations immunize your puppy against viruses.

DID YOU KNOW?

Dogs who have been exposed to lawns sprayed with herbicides have double and triple the rate of malignant lymphoma. Town dogs are especially at risk, as they are exposed to tailored lawns and gardens. Dogs perspire and absorb through their footpads. Be careful where your dog walks and always avoid any area that appears yellowed from chemical overspray.

The usual vaccines contain immunizing doses of several different viruses such as distemper, parvovirus, parainfluenza and hepatitis. There are other vaccines available when the puppy is at risk. You should rely upon professional advice. This is especially true for the booster-shot programme. Most vaccination programmes require a booster when the puppy is a year old and once a year thereafter. In some cases, circumstances may require more frequent immunizations. Kennel cough, more formally known as tracheobronchitis, is treated with a vaccine that is sprayed into the dog's nostrils. Kennel cough is usually included in routine vaccination, but this is often not so effective as for other major diseases.

WEANING TO FIVE MONTHS OLD
Puppies should be weaned by the time they are about two months old. A puppy that remains for at least eight weeks with its mother and litter mates usually adapts better to other dogs and people later in its life.

Some new owners have their puppy examined by a veterinary surgeon immediately, which is a good idea. Vaccination programmes usually begin when the puppy is very young.

The puppy will have its teeth examined and have its skeletal conformation and general health checked prior to certification by the veterinary surgeon. Puppies in certain breeds have problems with their kneecaps, cataracts and other eye problems, heart murmurs and undescended testicles. They may also have personality problems and your veterinary surgeon might have training in temperament evaluation.

FIVE MONTHS TO ONE YEAR

Unless you intend to breed or show your dog, neutering the puppy at six months of age is recommended. Discuss this with your veterinary surgeon; most professionals advise neutering the puppy. Neutering has proven to be extremely beneficial to both male and female puppies. Besides eliminating the possibility of pregnancy, it inhibits (but does not prevent) breast cancer in bitches and prostate cancer in male dogs. Under no circumstances should a bitch be spayed prior to her first season.

Your veterinary surgeon should provide your puppy with a thorough dental evaluation at six months of age, ascertaining whether all the permanent teeth have erupted properly. A home dental care regimen should be

Skin problems are hard to detect under the Bobtail's profuse coat. Take the time during grooming to check the skin and coat for any abnormalities, irritations or other signs of a problem.

initiated at six months, including brushing weekly and providing good dental devices (such as nylon bones). Regular dental care promotes healthy teeth, fresh breath and a longer life.

ONE TO SEVEN YEARS

Once a year, your grown dog should visit the vet for an examination and vaccination boosters. Some vets recommend blood tests, thyroid level check and dental evaluation to accompany these annual visits. A thorough clinical evaluation by the vet can provide critical background information for your dog. Blood tests are often performed at one year of age, and dental examinations around the third or fourth birthday. In the long run, quality preventive care for your pet can save money, teeth and lives.

DID YOU KNOW?

Caring for the puppy starts before the puppy is born by keeping the dam healthy and well-nourished. Most puppies have worms, even if they are not evident, so a worming programme is essential. The worms continually shed eggs except during their dormant stage, when they just rest in the tissues of the puppy. During this stage they are not evident during a routine examination.

SKIN PROBLEMS IN BOBTAILS

Veterinary surgeons are consulted by dog owners for skin problems more than any other group of diseases or maladies. Dogs' skin is almost as sensitive as human skin and both suffer almost the same ailments (though the occurrence of acne in dogs is rare!). For this reason, veterinary dermatology has developed into a speciality practised by many veterinary surgeons.

Since many skin problems have visual symptoms that are almost identical, it requires the skill of an experienced veterinary dermatologist to identify and cure many of the more severe skin disorders. Pet shops sell many treatments for skin problems but most of the treatments are directed at symptoms and not the underlying problem(s). If your dog is suffering from a skin disorder, you should seek professional assistance as quickly as possible. As with all diseases, the earlier a problem is identified and treated, the more successful is the cure.

HEREDITARY SKIN DISORDERS

Veterinary dermatologists are currently researching a number of skin disorders that are believed to have a hereditary basis. These inherited diseases are transmitted by both parents, who appear (phenotypically) normal but have a recessive gene for the disease, meaning that they carry, but are

HEALTH AND VACCINATION SCHEDULE

Age in Weeks:	6th	8th	10th	12th	14th	16th	20-24th	1 yr
Worm Control	✔	✔	✔	✔	✔	✔	✔	
Neutering								✔
Heartworm*		✔		✔		✔	✔	
Parvovirus	✔		✔		✔		✔	✔
Distemper		✔		✔		✔		✔
Hepatitis		✔		✔		✔		✔
Leptospirosis								✔
Parainfluenza	✔		✔		✔			✔
Dental Examination		✔					✔	✔
Complete Physical		✔					✔	✔
Coronavirus				✔			✔	✔
Kennel Cough	✔							
Hip Dysplasia								✔
Rabies*							✔	

Vaccinations are not instantly effective. It takes about two weeks for the dog's immunization system to develop antibodies. Most vaccinations require annual booster shots. Your veterinary surgeon should guide you in this regard.
*Not applicable in the United Kingdom

not affected by, the disease. These disease pose serious problems to breeders because in some instances there is no method of identifying carriers. Often the secondary diseases associated with these skin conditions are even more debilitating than the skin disorder, including cancers and respiratory problems; others can be lethal.

Amongst the known hereditary skin disorders, for which the mode of inheritance is known, are acrodermatitis, cutaneous asthenia (Ehlers-Danlos syndrome), sabaceous adenitis, which is reported in the Bobtail, cyclic hematopoiesis, dermatomyositis, IgA deficiency, colour dilution alopecia and nodular dermatofibrosis. Some of these disorders are limited to one or two breeds and others affect a large number of breeds. All inherited diseases must be diagnosed and treated by a veterinary specialist.

PARASITE BITES
Many of us are allergic to insect bites. The bites itch, erupt and may even become infected. Dogs have the same reaction to fleas, ticks and/or mites. When an insect lands on you, you have the chance to whisk it away with your hand. Unfortunately, when your dog is bitten by a flea, tick or mite, it can only scratch it away or bite it. By

the time the dog has been bitten, the parasite has done some of its damage. It may also have laid eggs to cause further problems in the near future. The itching from parasite bites is probably due to the saliva injected into the site when the parasite sucks the dog's blood.

AUTO-IMMUNE SKIN CONDITIONS

Auto-immune skin conditions are commonly referred to as being allergic to yourself, whilst allergies are usually inflammatory reactions to an outside stimulus. Auto-immune diseases cause serious damage to the tissues that are involved.

DID YOU KNOW?

Vaccines do not work all the time. Sometimes dogs are allergic to them and many times the antibodies, which are supposed to be stimulated by the vaccine, just are not produced. You should keep your dog in the veterinary clinic for an hour after it is vaccinated to be sure there are no allergic reactions.

DISEASE REFERENCE CHART

	What is it?	What causes it?	Symptoms
Leptospirosis	Severe disease that affects the internal organs; can be spread to people.	A bacterium, which is often carried by rodents, that enters through mucous membranes and spreads quickly throughout the body.	Range from fever, vomiting and loss of appetite in less severe cases to shock, irreversible kidney damage and possibly death in most severe cases.
Rabies	Potentially deadly virus that infects warm-blooded mammals. Not seen in United Kingdom.	Bite from a carrier of the virus, mainly wild animals.	1st stage: dog exhibits change in behaviour, fear. 2nd stage: dog's behaviour becomes more aggressive. 3rd stage: loss of coordination, trouble with bodily functions.
Parvovirus	Highly contagious virus, potentially deadly.	Ingestion of the virus, which is usually spread through the faeces of infected dogs.	Most common: severe diarrhoea. Also vomiting, fatigue, lack of appetite.
Kennel cough	Contagious respiratory infection.	Combination of types of bacteria and virus. Most common: *Bordetella bronchiseptica* bacteria and parainfluenza virus.	Chronic cough.
Distemper	Disease primarily affecting respiratory and nervous system.	Virus that is related to the human measles virus.	Mild symptoms such as fever, lack of appetite and mucous secretion progress to evidence of brain damage, 'hard pad.'
Hepatitis	Virus primarily affecting the liver.	Canine adenovirus type I (CAV-1). Enters system when dog breathes in particles.	Lesser symptoms include listlessness, diarrhoea, vomiting. More severe symptoms include 'blue-eye' (clumps of virus in eye).
Coronavirus	Virus resulting in digestive problems.	Virus is spread through infected dog's faeces.	Stomach upset evidenced by lack of appetite, vomiting, diarrhoea.

Normal hairs of a dog enlarged 200 times original size. The cuticle (outer covering) is clean and healthy. Unlike human hair that grows from the base, dog's hair also grows from the end, as shown in the inset. Scanning electron micrographs by Dr Dennis Kunkel, University of Hawaii.

The best known auto-immune disease is lupus, which affects people as well as dogs. The symptoms are variable and may affect the kidneys, bones, blood chemistry and skin. It can be fatal to both dogs and humans, though it is not thought to be transmissible. It is usually successfully treated with cortisone, prednisone or a similar corticosteroid, but extensive use of these drugs can have harmful side effects.

HOT SPOTS

Hot spots, or moist dermatitis, occur on many coated breeds, and the Bobtail is unfortunately no exception. The manifestation of the problem is the dog's tireless attack at a specific area of the body, the legs or rear quarters. They lick so intensively that they remove the hair and skin, leaving an ugly wound. Owners who notice their dogs' biting and chewing at their extremities or rear quarters should have the vet determine the cause. Hot spots are treatable with corticosteroids, given by a vet through injection and then followed up orally at home. Usually the area must be shaved and cleaned thoroughly for the hot spot to be effectively cured.

AIRBORNE ALLERGIES

An interesting allergy is pollen allergy. Humans have hay fever, rose fever and other fevers with which they suffer during the pollinating season. Many dogs suffer the same allergies. When the pollen count is high, your dog might suffer but don't expect him to sneeze and have a runny nose like a human would. Dogs react to pollen allergies the same way they react to fleas—they scratch and bite themselves.

Dogs, like humans, can be tested for allergens. Discuss the testing with your veterinary dermatologist.

DID YOU KNOW?

A dental examination is in order when the dog is between six months and one year of age so any permanent teeth that have erupted incorrectly can be corrected. It is important to begin a brushing routine, preferably using a two-sided brushing technique, whereby both sides of the tooth are brushed at the same time. Durable nylon and safe edible chews should be a part of your puppy's arsenal for good health, good teeth and pleasant breath. The vast majority of dogs three to four years old and older has diseases of the gums from lack of dental attention. Using the various types of dental chews can be very effective in controlling dental plaque.

FOOD PROBLEMS

FOOD ALLERGIES

Dogs are allergic to many foods that are best-sellers and highly recommended by breeders and veterinary surgeons. Changing the brand of food that you buy may not eliminate the problem if the element to which the dog is allergic is contained in the new brand.

Recognising a food allergy is difficult. Humans vomit or have rashes when they eat a food to which they are allergic. Dogs neither vomit nor (usually) develop a rash. They react in the same manner as they do to an airborne or flea allergy; they itch, scratch and bite. This makes the diagnosis extremely difficult. Whilst pollen allergies and parasite bites are usually seasonal, food allergies are year-round problems.

FOOD INTOLERANCE

Food intolerance is the inability of the dog to completely digest certain foods. Puppies that may have done very well on their mother's milk may not do well on cow's milk. The rest of this food intolerance may be loose bowels, passing gas and stomach pains. These are the only obvious symptoms of food intolerance and that makes diagnosis difficult.

TREATING FOOD PROBLEMS

It is possible to handle food allergies and food intolerance yourself. Put your dog on a diet that it has never had. Obviously if it has never eaten this new food it can't have been allergic or intolerant of it. Start with a single ingredient that is not in the dog's diet at the present time. Ingredients like chopped beef or fish are common in dogs' diets, so try something more exotic like rabbit, pheasant or even just vegetables. Keep the dog on this diet (with no additives) for a month. If the symptoms of food allergy or intolerance disappear, chances are your dog has a food allergy.

Don't think that the single ingredient cured the problem. You still must find a suitable diet and ascertain which ingredient in the old diet was objectionable. This is most easily done by adding ingredients to the new diet one at a time. Let the dog stay on the modified diet for a month before you add another ingredient. Eventually, you will determine the ingredient that caused the adverse reaction.

An alternative method is to carefully study the ingredients in the diet to which your dog is allergic or intolerant. Identify the main ingredient in this diet and eliminate the main ingredient by buying a different food that does not have that ingredient. Keep experimenting until the symptoms disappear after one month on the new diet.

First Aid at a Glance

Burns
Place the affected area under cool water; use ice if only a small area is burnt.

Bee/Insect bites
Apply ice to relieve swelling; antihistamine dosed properly.

Animal bites
Clean any bleeding area; apply pressure until bleeding subsides; go to the vet.

Spider bites
Use cold compress and a pressurised pack to inhibit venom's spreading.

Antifreeze poisoning
Induce vomiting with hydrogen peroxide. Seek *immediate* veterinary help!

Fish hooks
Removal best handled by vet; hook must be cut in order to remove.

Snake bites
Pack ice around bite; contact vet quickly; identify snake for proper antivenin.

Car accident
Move dog from roadway with blanket; seek veterinary aid.

Shock
Calm the dog, keep him warm; seek immediate veterinary help.

Nosebleed
Apply cold compress to the nose; apply pressure to any visible abrasion.

Bleeding
Apply pressure above the area; treat wound by applying a cotton pack.

Heat stroke
Submerge dog in cold bath; cool down with fresh air and water; go to the vet.

Frostbite/Hypothermia
Warm the dog with a warm bath, electric blankets or hot water bottles.

Abrasions
Clean the wound and wash out thoroughly with fresh water; apply antiseptic.

 Remember: an injured dog may attempt to bite a helping hand from fear and confusion. Always muzzle the dog before trying to offer assistance.

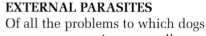

A scanning electron micrograph (S. E. M.) of a dog flea, *Ctenocephalides canis*.

Magnified head of a dog flea, *Ctenocephalides canis*.

A male dog flea, *Ctenocephalides canis*.

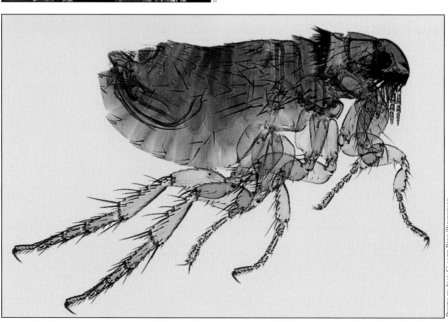

EXTERNAL PARASITES

Of all the problems to which dogs are prone, none is more well known and frustrating than fleas. Flea infestation is relatively simple to cure but difficult to prevent. Parasites that are harboured inside the body are a bit more difficult to eradicate but they are easier to control.

FLEAS

To control a flea infestation you have to understand the flea's life cycle. Fleas are often thought of as a summertime problem but centrally heated homes have changed the patterns and fleas can be found at any time of the year. The most effective method of flea control is a two-stage approach:

one stage to kill the adult fleas, and the other to control the development of pre-adult fleas. Unfortunately, no single active ingredient is effective against all stages of the life cycle.

LIFE CYCLE STAGES

During its life, a flea will pass through four life stages: egg, larva, pupa and adult. The adult stage is the most visible and irritating stage of the flea life cycle and this is why the majority of flea-control products concentrate on this stage. The fact is that adult fleas account for only 1% of the total flea population, and the other 99% exist in pre-adult stages, i.e. eggs, larvae and pupae. The pre-adult stages are barely visible to the naked eye.

THE LIFE CYCLE OF THE FLEA

Eggs are laid on the dog, usually in quantities of about 20 or 30, several times a day. The female adult flea must have a blood meal

before each egg-laying session. When first laid, the eggs will cling to the dog's fur, as the eggs are still moist. However, they will quickly dry out and fall from the dog, especially if the dog moves around or scratches. Many eggs will fall off in the dog's favourite area or an area in which he spends a lot of time, such as his bed.

Once the eggs fall from the dog onto the carpet or furniture, they will hatch into larvae. This takes from one to ten days. Larvae are not particularly mobile, and will usually travel only a few inches from where they hatch. However, they do have a tendency to move

ILLUSTRATION COURTESY OF BAYER VITAL GMBH & CO. KG

A Look at Fleas

Fleas have been around for millions of years and have adapted to changing host animals. They are able to go through a complete life cycle in less than one month or they can extend their lives to almost two years by remaining as pupae or cocoons. They do not need blood or any other food for up to 20 months.

They have been measured as being able to jump 300,000 times and can jump 150 times their length in any direction including straight up. Those are just a few of the reasons why they are so successful in infesting a dog!

away from light and heavy traffic—under furniture and behind doors are common places to find high quantities of flea larvae.

The flea larvae feed on dead organic matter, including adult flea faeces, until they are ready to change into adult fleas. Fleas will usually remain as larvae for around seven days. After this period, the larvae will pupate into protective pupae. While inside the pupae, the larvae will undergo metamorphosis and change into adult fleas. This can take as little time as a few days, but the adult fleas can remain inside the pupae waiting to hatch for up to two years. The pupae are signalled to hatch by certain stimuli, such as physical pressure—the pupae's being stepped on, heat from an animal lying on the pupae or increased carbon dioxide levels and vibrations—indicating that a suitable host is available.

Once hatched, the adult flea must feed within a few days. Once the adult flea finds a host, it will not leave voluntarily. It only becomes dislodged by grooming or

---

EN GARDE: CATCHING FLEAS OFF GUARD

Consider the following ways to arm yourself against fleas:
• Add a small amount of pennyroyal or eucalyptus oil to your dog's bath. These natural remedies repel fleas.
• Supplement your dog's food with fresh garlic (minced or grated) and a hearty amount of brewer's yeast, both of which ward off fleas.
• Use a flea comb on your dog daily. Submerge fleas in a cup of bleach to kill them quickly.
• Confine the dog to only a few rooms to limit the spread of fleas in the home.
• Vacuum daily...and get all of the crevices! Dispose of the bag every few days until the problem is under control.
• Wash your dog's bedding daily. Cover cushions where your dog sleeps with towels, and wash the towels often.

DID YOU KNOW?

Never mix flea control products without first consulting your veterinary surgeon. Some products can become toxic when combined with others and can cause serious or fatal consequences.

---

the host animal's scratching. The adult flea will remain on the host for the duration of its life unless forcibly removed.

TREATING THE ENVIRONMENT AND THE DOG

Treating fleas should be a two-pronged attack. First, the environment needs to be treated; this includes carpets and furniture, especially the dog's bedding and

Opposite page: A scanning electron micrograph of a dog or cat flea, *Ctenocephalides*, magnified more than 100x. This image has been colorized for effect.

The Life Cycle of the Flea

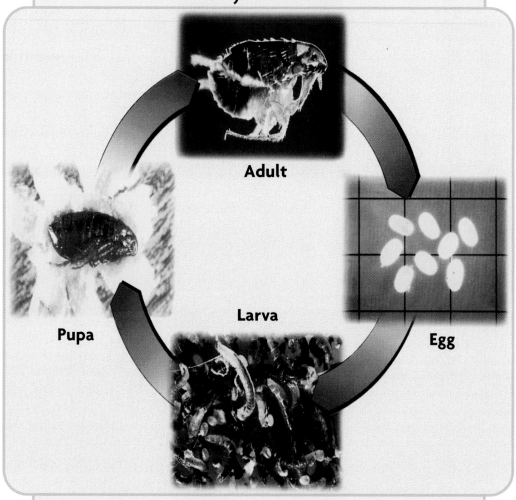

Adult

Egg

Larva

Pupa

This graphic depiction of the life cycle of the flea appears courtesy of Fleabusters®, Rx for fleas.

areas underneath furniture. The environment should be treated with a household spray containing an Insect Growth Regulator (IGR) and an insecticide to kill the adult fleas. Most IGRs are effective against eggs and larvae; they actually mimic the fleas' own hormones and stop the eggs and larvae from developing into adult fleas. There are currently no treatments available to attack the pupa stage of the life cycle, so the adult insecticide is used to kill the newly hatched adult fleas before

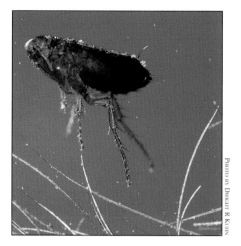

Photo by Dwight R Kuhn

TICKS AND MITES

Though not as common as fleas, ticks and mites are found all over the tropical and temperate world. They don't bite, like fleas; they harpoon. They dig their sharp proboscis (nose) into the dog's skin and drink the blood. Their only food and drink is dog's blood. Dogs can get Lyme disease, Rocky Mountain spotted fever (normally

Dwight R Kuhn's magnificent action photo showing a flea jumping from a dog's back.

they find a host. Most IGRs are active for many months, whilst adult insecticides are only active for a few days.

When treating with a household spray, it is a good idea to vacuum before applying the product. This stimulates as many pupae as possible to hatch into adult fleas. The vacuum cleaner should also be treated with a flea treatment to prevent the eggs and larvae that have been hoovered into the vacuum bag from hatching.

The second stage of treatment is to apply an adult insecticide to the dog. Traditionally, this would be in the form of a collar or a spray, but more recent innovations include digestible insecticides that poison the fleas when they ingest the dog's blood. Alternatively, there are drops that, when placed on the back of the animal's neck, spread throughout the fur and skin to kill adult fleas.

FLEA CONTROL

Two types of products should be used when treating fleas—a product to treat the pet and a product to treat the home. Adult fleas represent less than 1% of the flea population. The pre-adult fleas (eggs, larvae and pupae) represent more than 99% of the flea population and are found in the environment; it is in the case of pre-adult fleas that products containing an Insect Growth Regulator (IGR) should be used in the home.

IGRs are a new class of compounds used to prevent the development of insects. They do not kill the insect outright, but instead use the insect's biology against it to stop it from completing its growth. Products that contain methoprene are the world's first and leading IGRs. Used to control fleas and other insects, this type of IGR will stop flea larvae from developing and protect the house for up to seven months.

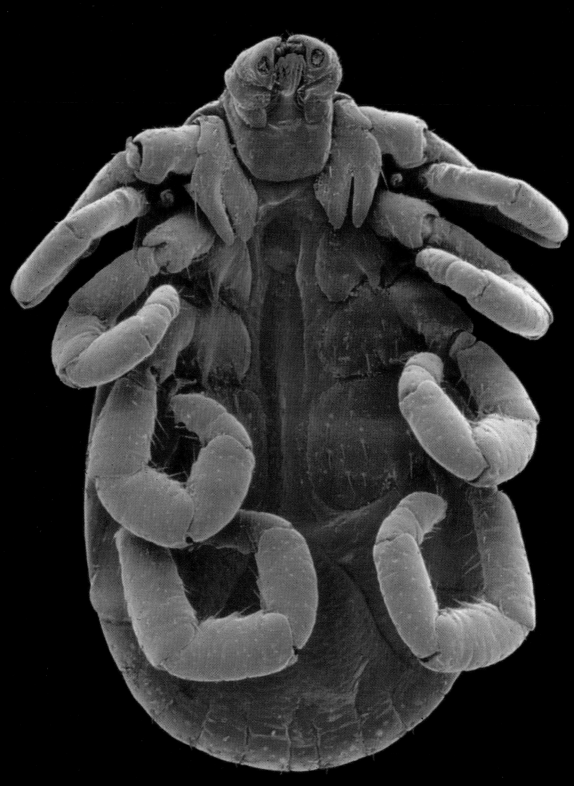

found in the US only), paralysis and many other diseases from ticks and mites. They may live where fleas are found and they like to hide in cracks or seams in walls wherever dogs live. They are controlled the same way fleas are controlled.

The dog tick, *Dermacentor variabilis*, may well be the most common dog tick in many geographical areas, especially those areas where the climate is hot and humid.

Most dog ticks have life expectancies of a week to six

ILLUSTRATION COURTESY OF BAYER VITAL GMBH & CO. KG

Beware the Deer Tick

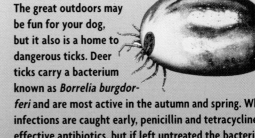

The great outdoors may be fun for your dog, but it also is a home to dangerous ticks. Deer ticks carry a bacterium known as *Borrelia burgdorferi* and are most active in the autumn and spring. When infections are caught early, penicillin and tetracycline are effective antibiotics, but if left untreated the bacteria may cause neurological, kidney and cardiac problems as well as long-term trouble with walking and painful joints.

A deer tick, the carrier of Lyme disease. This magnified micrograph has been colourized for effect.

Opposite page: The dog tick, *Dermacentor variabilis*, is probably the most common tick found on dogs. Look at the strength in its eight legs! No wonder it's hard to detach them.

S. E. M. BY DR ANDREW SPIELMAN/PHOTOTAKE

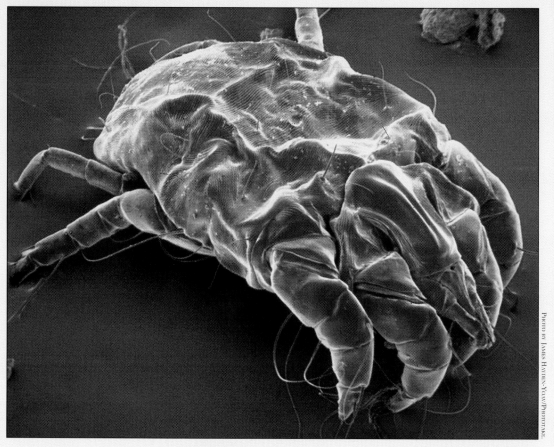

**Above:
The mange mite,
Psoroptes bovis.**

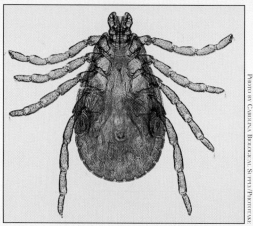

A brown dog tick, *Rhipicephalus sanguineus*, is
an uncommon but annoying tick found on dogs.

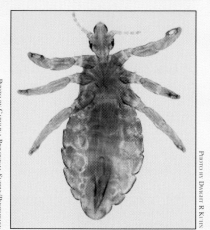

Human lice look like dog lice;
the two are closely related.

months, depending upon climatic conditions. They can neither jump nor fly, but they can crawl slowly and can range up to 5 metres (16 feet) to reach a sleeping or unsuspecting dog.

MANGE

Mites cause a skin irritation called mange. Some are contagious, like *Cheyletiella*, ear mites, scabies and chiggers. Mites that cause ear-mite infestations are usually controlled with Lindane, which can only be administered by a vet, followed by Tresaderm at home.

It is essential that your dog be treated for mange as quickly as possible because some forms of mange are transmissible to people.

INTERNAL PARASITES

Most animals—fishes, birds and mammals, including dogs and humans—have worms and other parasites that live inside their bodies. According to Dr Herbert R Axelrod, the fish pathologist, there are two kinds of parasites: dumb and smart. The smart parasites live in peaceful cooperation with their hosts (symbiosis), while the dumb parasites kill their host. Most of the worm infections are relatively easy to control. If they are not controlled they weaken the host dog to the point that other medical problems occur, but they are not dumb parasites.

ROUNDWORMS

The roundworms that infect dogs are scientifically known as *Toxocara canis*. They live in the dog's intestine. The worms shed eggs continually. It has been estimated that a dog produces about 150 grammes of faeces every day. Each gramme of faeces averages 10,000–12,000 eggs of roundworms. There are no known areas in which dogs roam that do not contain roundworm eggs. The greatest danger of roundworms is that they infect people too! It is

DEWORMING

Ridding your puppy of worms is VERY IMPORTANT because certain worms that puppies carry, such as tapeworms and roundworms, can infect humans.

Breeders initiate a deworming programme at or about four weeks of age. The routine is repeated every two or three weeks until the puppy is three months old. The breeder from whom you obtained your puppy should provide you with the complete details of the deworming programme.

Your veterinary surgeon can prescribe and monitor the programme of deworming for you. The usual programme is treating the puppy every 15–20 days until the puppy is positively worm free.

It is not advised that you treat your puppy with drugs that are not recommended professionally.

ROUNDWORMS

Average size dogs can pass 1,360,000 roundworm eggs every day.

For example, if there were only 1 million dogs in the world, the world would be saturated with 1,300 metric tonnes of dog faeces.

These faeces would contain 15,000,000,000 roundworm eggs.

It's known that 7–31% of home gardens and children's play boxes in the US contain roundworm eggs.

Flushing dog's faeces down the toilet is not a safe practice because the usual sewage treatments do not destroy roundworm eggs.

Infected puppies start shedding roundworm eggs at 3 weeks of age. They can be infected by their mother's milk.

wise to have your dog tested regularly for roundworms.

Pigs also have roundworm infections that can be passed to humans and dogs. The typical roundworm parasite is called *Ascaris lumbricoides.*

HOOKWORMS

The worm *Ancylostoma caninum* is commonly called the dog hookworm. It is dangerous to humans and cats. It also has teeth by which it attaches itself to the intestines of the dog. It changes the site of its attachment about six times a day and the dog loses blood from each detachment, possibly causing iron-deficiency anaemia. Hookworms are easily purged from the dog with many medications. Milbemycin oxime,

The roundworm, *Rhabditis.* The roundworm can infect both dogs and humans.

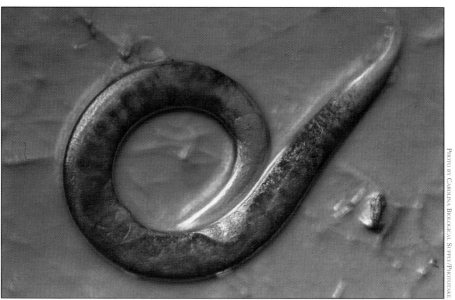

PHOTO BY CAROLINA BIOLOGICAL SUPPLY/PHOTOTAKE

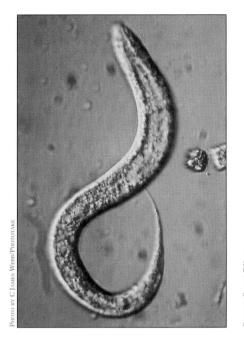

PHOTO BY C JAMES WEBB/PHOTOTAKE

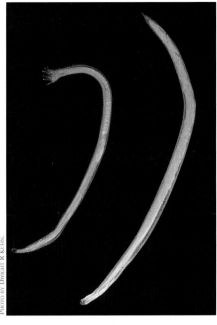

PHOTO BY DWIGHT R KUHN.

Left:
The infective
stage of the
hookworm larva.

Right:
Male and female
hookworms,
*Ancylostoma
caninum*, are
uncommonly
found in pet or
show dogs in
Britain.
Hookworms may
infect other dogs
that have exposure
to grasslands.

which also serves as a heartworm preventative in Collies, can be used for this purpose.

In Britain the 'temperate climate' hookworm (*Uncinaria stenocephala*) is rarely found in pet or show dogs, but can occur in hunting packs, racing Greyhounds and sheepdogs because the worms can be prevalent wherever dogs are exercised regularly on grassland.

TAPEWORMS

There are many species of tapeworms. They are carried by fleas! The dog eats the flea and starts the tapeworm cycle. Humans can also be infected with tapeworms, so don't eat fleas! Fleas are so small that your dog could

pass them onto your hands, your plate or your food and thus make it possible for you to ingest a flea which is carrying tapeworm eggs.

While tapeworm infection is not life threatening in dogs (smart parasite!), it can be the cause of a

DID YOU KNOW?

Never allow your dog to swim in polluted water or public areas where water quality can be suspect. Even perfectly clear water can harbour parasites, many of which can cause serious to fatal illnesses in canines. Areas inhabited by waterfowl and other wildlife are especially dangerous.

137

The head and rostellum (the round prominence on the scolex) of a tapeworm, which infects dogs and humans.

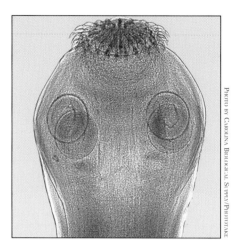

PHOTO BY CAROLINA BIOLOGICAL SUPPLY/PHOTOTAKE

very serious liver disease for humans. About 50 percent of the humans infected with *Echinococcus multilocularis*, a type of tapeworm that causes alveolar hydatis, perish.

HEARTWORMS

Heartworms are thin, extended worms up to 30 cms (12 ins) long which live in a dog's heart and the major blood vessels surrounding it. Dogs may have up to 200 worms. Symptoms may be loss of energy, loss of appetite, coughing, the development of a pot belly and anaemia.

Heartworms are transmitted by mosquitoes. The mosquito drinks the blood of an infected dog and takes in larvae with the blood. The larvae, called microfilaria, develop within the body of the mosquito and are passed on to the next dog bitten after the larvae mature. It takes two to three weeks for the

TAPEWORMS

Humans, rats, squirrels, foxes, coyotes, wolves, mixed breeds of dogs and purebred dogs are all susceptible to tapeworm infection. Except in humans, tapeworms are usually not a fatal infection.

Infected individuals can harbour a thousand parasitic worms.

Tapeworms have two sexes—male and female (many other worms have only one sex—male and female in the same worm).

If dogs eat infected rats or mice, they get the tapeworm disease.

One month after attaching to a dog's intestine, the worm starts shedding eggs. These eggs are infective immediately.

Infective eggs can live for a few months without a host animal.

Roundworms, whipworms and hookworms are just a few of the other commonly known worms that infect dogs.

larvae to develop to the infective stage within the body of the mosquito. Dogs should be treated at about six weeks of age, and maintained on a prophylactic dose given monthly.

Blood testing for heartworms is not necessarily indicative of how seriously your dog is infected. This is a dangerous disease. Although heartworm is a problem for dogs in America, Australia, Asia and Central Europe, dogs in the United Kingdom are not currently affected by heartworm.

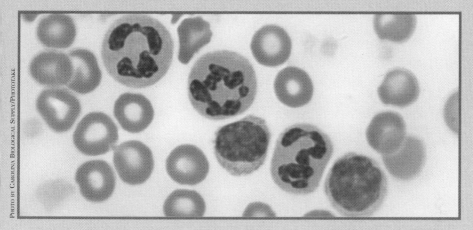

Magnified
heartworm
larvae,
*Dirofilaria
immitis.*

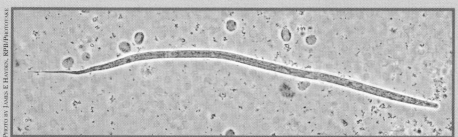

The heartworm,
Dirofilaria immitis.

The heart
of a dog infected
with canine
heartworm,
*Dirofilaria
immitis.*

HOMEOPATHY:
an alternative to medicine

'Less is Most'

Using this principle, the strength of a homeopathic remedy is measured by the number of serial dilutions that were undertaken to create it. The greater the number of serial dilutions, the greater the strength of the homeopathic remedy. The potency of a remedy that has been made by making a dilution of 1 part in 100 parts (or 1/100) is 1c or 1cH. If this remedy is subjected to a series of further dilutions, each one being 1/100, a more dilute and stronger remedy is produced. If the remedy is diluted in this way six times, it is called 6c or 6cH. A dilution of 6c is 1 part in 1000,000,000,000. In general, higher potencies in more frequent doses are better for acute symptoms and lower potencies in more infrequent doses are more useful for chronic, long-standing problems.

CURING OUR DOGS NATURALLY

Holistic medicine means treating the whole animal as a unique, perfect living being. Generally, holistic treatments do not suppress the symptoms that the body naturally produces, as do most medications prescribed by conventional doctors and vets. Holistic methods seek to cure disease by regaining balance and harmony in the patient's environment. Some of these methods include use of nutritional therapy, herbs, flower essences, aromatherapy, acupuncture, massage, chiropractic, and, of course the most popular holistic approach, homeopathy. Homeopathy is a theory or system of treating illness with small doses of substances which, if administered in larger quantities, would produce the symptoms that the patient already has. This approach is often described as 'like cures like.' Although modern veterinary medicine is geared toward the 'quick fix,' homeopathy relies on the belief that, given the time, the body is able to heal itself and return to its natural, healthy state.

Choosing a remedy to cure a problem in our dogs is the difficult part of homeopathy. Consult with your veterinary surgeon for a professional diagnosis of your dog's symptoms. Often these symptoms require immediate conventional care. If your vet is willing, and somewhat knowledgeable, you may attempt a homeopathic remedy. Be aware that cortisone prevents homeopathic remedies from working. There are hundreds of possibilities and combinations to cure many problems in dogs, from basic physical problems such as excessive moulting, fleas or other parasites, unattractive doggy odour, bad breath, upset tummy, dry, oily or dull coat, diarrhoea, ear problems or eye discharge (including tears and dry or mucousy matter), to behavioural abnormalities, such as fear of loud noises, habitual licking, poor appetite, excessive barking, obesity and various phobias. From alumina to zincum metallicum, the remedies span the planet and the imagination…from flowers and weeds to chemicals, insect droppings, diesel smoke and volcanic ash.

Using 'Like to Treat Like'

Unlike conventional medicines that suppress symptoms, homeopathic remedies treat illnesses with small doses of substances that, if administered in larger quantities, would produce the symptoms that the patient already has. Whilst the same homeopathic remedy can be used to treat different symptoms in different dogs, here are some interesting remedies and their uses.

Apis Mellifica
(made from honey bee venom) can be used for allergies or to reduce swelling that occurs in acutely infected kidneys.

Diesel Smoke
can be used to help control travel sickness.

Calcarea Fluorica
(made from calcium fluoride which helps harden bone structure) can be useful in treating hard lumps in tissues.

Natrum Muriaticum
(made from common salt, sodium chloride) is useful in treating thin, thirsty dogs.

Nitricum Acidum
(made from nitric acid) is used for symptoms you would expect to see from contact with acids such as lesions, especially where the skin joins the linings of body orifices or openings such as the lips and nostrils.

Symphytum
(made from the herb Knitbone, Symphytum officianale) is used to encourage bones to heal.

Urtica Urens
(made from the common stinging nettle) is used in treating painful, irritating rashes.

HOMEOPATHIC REMEDIES FOR YOUR DOG

Symptom/Ailment	Possible Remedy
ALLERGIES	Apis Mellifica 30c, Astacus Fluviatilis 6c, Pulsatilla 30c, Urtica Urens 6c
ALOPECIA	Alumina 30c, Lycopodium 30c, Sepia 30c, Thallium 6c
ANAL GLANDS (BLOCKED)	Hepar Sulphuris Calcareum 30c, Sanicula 6c, Silicea 6c
ARTHRITIS	Rhus Toxicodendron 6c, Bryonia Alba 6c
CATARACT	Calcarea Carbonica 6c, Conium Maculatum 6c, Phosphorus 30c, Silicea 30c
CONSTIPATION	Alumina 6c, Carbo Vegetabilis 30c, Graphites 6c, Nitricum Acidum 30c, Silicea 6c
COUGHING	Aconitum Napellus 6c, Belladonna 30c, Hyoscyamus Niger 30c, Phosphorus 30c
DIARRHOEA	Arsenicum Album 30c, Aconitum Napellus 6c, Chamomilla 30c, Mercurius Corrosivus 30c
DRY EYE	Zincum Metallicum 30c
EAR PROBLEMS	Aconitum Napellus 30c, Belladonna 30c, Hepar Sulphuris 30c, Tellurium 30c, Psorinum 200c
EYE PROBLEMS	Borax 6c, Aconitum Napellus 30c, Graphites 6c, Staphysagria 6c, Thuja Occidentalis 30c
GLAUCOMA	Aconitum Napellus 30c, Apis Mellifica 6c, Phosphorus 30c
HEAT STROKE	Belladonna 30c, Gelsemium Sempervirens 30c, Sulphur 30c
HICCOUGHS	Cinchona Deficinalis 6c
HIP DYSPLASIA	Colocynthis 6c, Rhus Toxicodendron 6c, Bryonia Alba 6c
INCONTINENCE	Argentum Nitricum 6c, Causticum 30c, Conium Maculatum 30c, Pulsatilla 30c, Sepia 30c
INSECT BITES	Apis Mellifica 30c, Cantharis 30c, Hypericum Perforatum 6c, Urtica Urens 30c
ITCHING	Alumina 30c, Arsenicum Album 30c, Carbo Vegetabilis 30c, Hypericum Perforatum 6c, Mezerium 6c, Sulphur 30c
KENNEL COUGH	Drosera 6c, Ipecacuanha 30c
MASTITIS	Apis Mellifica 30c, Belladonna 30c, Urtica Urens 1m
PATELLAR LUXATION	Gelsemium Sempervirens 6c, Rhus Toxicodendron 6c
PENIS PROBLEMS	Aconitum Napellus 30c, Hepar Sulphuris Calcareum 30c, Pulsatilla 30c, Thuja Occidentalis 6c
PUPPY TEETHING	Calcarea Carbonica 6c, Chamomilla 6c, Phytolacca 6c
TRAVEL SICKNESS	Cocculus 6c, Petroleum 6c

Recognising a Sick Dog

Unlike colicky babies and cranky children, our canine kids cannot tell us when they are feeling ill. Therefore, there are a number of signs that owners can identify to know that their dogs are not feeling well.

Take note for physical manifestations such as:

- unusual, bad odour, including bad breath
- excessive moulting
- wax in the ears, chronic ear irritation
- oily, flaky, dull haircoat
- mucous, tearing or similar discharge in the eyes
- fleas or mites
- mucous in stool, diarrhoea
- sensitivity to petting or handling
- licking at paws, scratching face, etc.

Keep an eye out for behavioural changes as well including:

- lethargy, idleness
- lack of patience or general irritability
- lack of appetite, digestive problems
- phobias (fear of people, loud noises, etc.)
- strange behaviour, suspicion, fear
- coprophagia
- more frequent barking
- whimpering, crying

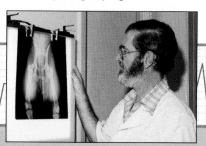

Get Well Soon

You don't need a DVR or a BVMA to provide good TLC to your sick or recovering dog, but you do need to pay attention to some details that normally wouldn't bother him. The following tips will aid Fido's recovery and get him back on his paws again:

- Keep his space free of irritating smells, like heavy perfumes and air fresheners.
- Rest is the best medicine! Avoid harsh lighting that will prevent your dog from sleeping. Shade him from bright sunlight during the day and dim the lights in the evening.
- Keep the noise level down. Animals are more sensitive to sound when they are sick.

- Be attentive to any necessary temperature adjustments. A dog with a fever needs a cool room and cold liquids. A bitch that is whelping or recovering from surgery will be more comfortable in a warm room, consuming warm liquids and food.
- You wouldn't send a sick child back to school early, so don't rush your dog back into a full routine until he seems absolutely ready.

The term 'old' is a qualitative term. For dogs, as well as their masters, old is relative. Certainly we can all distinguish between a puppy Bobtail and an adult Bobtail—there are the obvious physical traits, such as size, appearance and facial expressions, and personality traits. Puppies that are nasty are very rare. Puppies and young dogs like to play with children. Children's natural exuberance is a good match for the seemingly endless energy of young dogs. They like to run, jump, chase and retrieve. When dogs grow up and cease their interaction with children, they are often thought of as being too old to play with the kids.

On the other hand, if a Bobtail is only exposed to people over 60 years of age, its life will normally be less active and it will not seem to be getting old as its activity level slows down.

If people live to be 100 years old, dogs live to be 20 years old. Whilst this is a good rule of thumb, it is very inaccurate. When trying to compare dog years to human years, you cannot make a generalisation about all dogs. You can make the generalisation that 12 years is a good lifespan for a Bobtail, which is quite good compared to many other purebred dogs that may only live to 8 or 9 years of age. Some Bobtails have been known to live to 15 years. Dogs are generally considered mature within three years, but they can reproduce even earlier. So the first three years of a dog's life are like seven times that of comparable humans. That means a 3-year-old dog is like a 21-year-old human. As the curve of comparison shows, there is no hard and fast rule for comparing dog and human ages. The comparison is made even more difficult, for not all humans age at the same rate...and human females live longer than human males.

WHAT TO LOOK FOR IN SENIORS

Most veterinary surgeons and behaviourists use the seventh year mark as the time to consider a dog a 'senior.' The term 'senior' does not imply that the dog is geriatric and has begun to fail in mind and body. Ageing is essentially a slowing process. Humans readily admit that they feel a difference in their activity level from age 20 to 30, and then from 30 to 40, etc. By treating the seven-year-old dog as a senior, owners are able to implement certain therapeutic and preventative medical strategies with the help of their veterinary surgeons. A senior care programme should include at least two veterinary visits per year, screening sessions to determine the dog's health status, as well as nutritional counselling. Veterinary surgeons determine the senior dog's health status through a blood smear for a complete blood count, serum chemistry profile with electrolytes, urinalysis, blood pressure check, electrocardiogram, ocular tonometry (pressure on the eyeball) and dental prophylaxis.

Such an extensive programme for senior dogs is well advised before owners start to see the obvious physical signs of ageing, such as slower and inhibited movement, greying, increased sleep/nap periods and disinterest in play and other activity. This preventative programme promises a longer, healthier life for the ageing dog. Amongst the physical problems common in ageing dogs are the loss of sight and hearing, arthritis, kidney and liver failure, diabetes mellitus, heart disease and Cushing's disease (a hormonal disease).

In addition to the physical manifestations discussed, there are some behavioural changes and problems related to ageing dogs. Dogs suffering from hearing or vision loss, dental discomfort or arthritis can become aggressive. Likewise the near-deaf and/or blind dog may be startled more easily and react in an unexpectedly aggressive manner. Seniors suffering from senility can become more impatient and irritable. Housesoiling accidents are associated with loss of mobility, kidney problems, loss of sphincter control as well as plaque accumulation, physiological brain changes and reactions to medications. Older dogs, just like young puppies, suffer from separation anxiety, which can lead to excessive barking, whining, housesoiling and destructive behaviour. Seniors may become fearful of everyday sounds, such as vacuum cleaners, heaters, thunder and passing traffic. Some dogs have difficulty sleeping, due to discomfort, the need for frequent toilet visits and the like.

Owners should avoid spoiling the older dog with too many fatty treats. Obesity is a common problem in older dogs and subtracts years from their lifespan. Keep the senior dog as trim as possible since excessive weight puts additional stress on the body's vital organs. Some breeders recommend supplementing the diet with foods high in fibre and lower in calories. Adding fresh vegetables and marrow broth to the senior's diet makes a tasty, low-calorie, low-fat supplement. Vets also offer speciality diets for senior dogs that are worth exploring.

Your dog, as he nears his twilight years, needs his owner's patience and good care more than ever. Never punish an older dog for an accident or abnormal behaviour. For all the years of love, protection and companionship that your dog has provided, he deserves special attention and courtesies. The older dog may need to relieve himself at 3 a.m. because he can no longer hold it for eight hours. Older dogs may not be able to remain crated for more than two or three hours. It may be time to give up a sofa or chair to your old friend. Although he may not seem as enthusiastic about your attention and petting, he does appreciate the considerations you offer as he gets older.

Your Bobtail does not understand why his world is slowing down. Owners must make the transition into the golden years as pleasant and rewarding as possible.

WHAT TO DO WHEN THE TIME COMES

You are never fully prepared to make a rational decision about putting your dog to sleep. It is very obvious that you love your Bobtail or you would not be reading this book. Putting a loved dog to sleep is extremely difficult. It is a decision that must be made with your veterinary surgeon. You are usually forced to make the decision when one of the life-threatening symptoms listed above becomes serious enough for you to seek medical (veterinary) help.

If the prognosis of the malady indicates the end is near and your beloved pet will only suffer more and experience no enjoyment for the balance of its life, then euthanasia is the right choice.

WHAT IS EUTHANASIA?

Euthanasia derives from the Greek meaning *good death*. In other words, it means the planned, painless killing of a dog suffering from a painful, incurable condition, or who is so aged that it cannot walk, see, eat or control its excretory functions.

Euthanasia is usually accomplished by injection with an overdose of an anaesthesia or barbiturate. Aside from the prick of the needle, the experience is usually painless.

MAKING THE DECISION

The decision to euthanise your dog is never easy. The days during which the dog becomes ill and the end occurs can be unusually stressful for you. If this is your first experience with the death of a loved one, you may need the comfort dictated by your religious beliefs. If you are the head of the family and have children, you should have involved them in the decision of putting your Bobtail to sleep. Usually your dog can be maintained on drugs for a few days in order to give you ample time to make a decision. During this time, talking with members of your family or even people who have lived through this same experience can ease the burden of your inevitable decision.

THE FINAL RESTING PLACE

Dogs can have some of the same privileges as humans. The remains of your beloved dog can be buried in a pet cemetery, which is generally expensive. Dogs who have died at home can be buried in your garden in a place suitably marked with some stone or newly planted tree or bush. Alternatively, they can be cremated individually and the ashes returned to you. A less expensive option is mass cremation, although, of course, the ashes can not then be returned. Vets can usually arrange the cremation on your behalf. In Britain if your dog has died at the surgery, the vet legally cannot allow you to take your dog's body home. The cost of these options should always be discussed frankly and openly with your veterinary surgeon.

GETTING ANOTHER DOG?

The grief of losing your beloved dog will be as lasting as the grief of losing a human friend or relative. In most cases, if your dog died of old age (if there is such a thing), it had slowed down considerably. Do you want a new Bobtail puppy to replace it? Or are you better off

Your veterinary surgeon can most likely recommend a final resting place for your beloved Old English Sheepdog.

finding a more mature Bobtail, say two to three years of age, which will usually be housetrained and will have an already developed personality. In this case, you can find out if you like each other after a few hours of being together.

The decision is, of course, your own. Do you want another Bobtail or perhaps a different breed so as to avoid comparison with your beloved friend? Most people usually buy the same breed because they know (and love) the characteristics of that breed. Then, too, they often know people who have the same breed and perhaps they are lucky enough that one of their friends expects a litter soon. What could be better?

When you purchased your Bobtail you should have made it clear to the breeder whether you wanted one just as a loveable companion and pet, or if you hoped to be buying a Bobtail with show prospects. No reputable breeder will sell you a young puppy saying that it is definitely of show quality, for so much can go wrong during the early weeks and

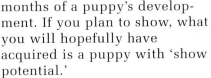

DID YOU KNOW?

You can get information about dog shows from kennel clubs and breed clubs:

Fédération Cynologique Internationale
14, rue Leopold II, B-6530 Thuin, Belgium
www.fci.be

The Kennel Club
1-5 Clarges St., Piccadilly
London W1Y 8AB, UK
www.the-kennel-club.org.uk

American Kennel Club
5580 Centerview Drive
Raleigh, NC 27606-3390, USA
www.akc.org

Canadian Kennel Club
89 Skyway Ave., Suite 100
Etobicoke, Ontario
M9W 6R4 Canada
www.ckc.ca

months of a puppy's development. If you plan to show, what you will hopefully have acquired is a puppy with 'show potential.'

To the novice, exhibiting a Bobtail in the show ring may look easy but it usually takes a lot of hard work and devotion to do top winning at a show such as the prestigious Crufts, not to mention a little luck too!

The first concept that the canine novice learns when watching a dog show is that each dog first competes against members of its own breed. Once the judge has selected the best member of each breed, provided that the show is judged on a Group system, that chosen dog will compete with other dogs in its group. Finally the best of each group will compete for Best in Show and Reserve Best in Show.

The second concept that you must understand is that the dogs are not actually competing against one another. The judge compares each dog against the breed standard, which is a written description of the ideal specimen of the breed. While some early breed

standards were indeed based on specific dogs that were famous or popular, many dedicated enthusiasts say that a perfect specimen, described in the standard, has never been bred. Thus the 'perfect' dog never walked into a show ring and, to the woe of dog breeders around the globe, does not exist. Breeders attempt to get as close to this ideal as possible, with every litter, but theoretically the 'perfect' dog is so elusive that it is impossible. (And if the 'perfect' dog were born, breeders and judges would never agree that it was indeed 'perfect.')

If you are interested in exploring dog shows, your best bet is to join your local breed club. These clubs often host both Championship and Open Shows, and sometimes Match meetings and Special Events, all of which could be of interest, even if you are only an onlooker. Clubs also send out newsletters and some organise training days and seminars in order that people may learn more about their chosen breed. To locate the breed club closest to you, contact The Kennel Club, the ruling body for the British dog world. The Kennel Club governs not only conformation shows but also working trials, obedience trials, agility trials and field trials. The

Kennel Club furnishes the rules and regulations for all these events plus general dog registration and other basic requirements of dog ownership. Its annual show, called the Crufts Dog Show, held in Birmingham, is the largest benched show in England. Every year over 20,000 of the UK's best dogs qualify to participate in this marvellous show which lasts four days.

The Kennel Club governs many different kinds of shows in Great Britain, Australia, South Africa and beyond. At the most competitive and prestigious of these shows, the Championship Shows, a dog can earn Challenge Certificates (CC's), and thereby become a

Show Champion or a Champion. A dog must earn three Challenge Certificates under three different judges to earn the prefix of 'Sh Ch' or 'Ch.' Note that some breeds must also qualify in a field trial in order to gain the title of full champion. Challenge Certificates are awarded to a very small percentage of the dogs competing, especially as dogs which are already Champions compete with others for these coveted CCs. The number of Challenge Certificates awarded in any one year is based upon the total number of dogs in each breed entered for competition. There are three types of Championship Shows: an all-breed General Championship Show for all Kennel-Club-recognised breeds; a Group Championship Show that is limited to breeds within one of the groups; and a Breed Show that is usually confined to a single breed. The Kennel Club determines which breeds at which Championship Shows will have the opportunity to earn Challenge Certificates (or tickets). Serious exhibitors often will opt not to participate if the tickets are withheld at a particular show. This policy makes earning championships even more difficult to accomplish.

Open Shows are generally

CLASSES AT DOG SHOWS

There can be as many as 18 classes per sex for your breed. Check the show schedule carefully to make sure that you have entered your dog in the appropriate class. Among the classes offered can be: Beginners; Minor Puppy (ages 6 to 9 months); Puppy (ages 6 to 12 months); Junior (ages 6 to 18 months); Beginners (handler or dog never won first place) as well as the following, each of which is defined in the schedule: Maiden; Novice; Tyro; Debutant; Undergraduate; Graduate; Postgraduate; Minor Limit; Mid Limit; Limit; Open; Veteran; Stud Dog; Brood Bitch; Progeny; Brace and Team.

less competitive and are frequently used as 'practice shows' for young dogs. There are hundreds of Open Shows each year that can be delightful social events and are great first show experiences for the novice. Even if you're considering just watching a show to wet your paws, an Open Show is a great choice.

While Championship and Open Shows are most important for the beginner to understand, there are other types of shows in which the interested dog owner can participate. Training clubs sponsor Matches that can be entered on the day of the show for a nominal fee. In these introductory-level exhibitions, two dogs are pulled out of a hat and 'matched,' the winner of that match goes on to the next round, and eventually only one dog is left undefeated.

Exemption Shows are much more light-hearted affairs with usually only four pedigree classes and several 'fun' classes, all of which can be entered on the day. Exemption Shows are sometimes held in conjunction with small agricultural shows and the proceeds must be given to a charity. Limited Shows are also available in small number, but entry is restricted to members of the club which hosts the show, although one can usually join the club when

HOW TO ENTER A DOG SHOW

1. Obtain an entry form and show schedule from the Show Secretary.
2. Select the classes that you want to enter and complete the entry form.
3. Transfer your dog into your name at The Kennel Club. (Be sure that this matter is handled before entering.)
4. Find out how far in advance show entries must be made. Oftentimes it's more than a couple of months.

WINNING THE TICKET

Earning a championship at Kennel Club shows is the most difficult in the world. Compared to the United States and Canada where it is relatively not 'challenging,' collecting three green tickets not only requires much time and effort, it can be very expensive!

Challenge Certificates, as the tickets are properly known, are the building blocks of champions—good breeding, good handling, good training and good luck!

making an entry.

Before you actually step into the ring, you would be well advised to sit back and observe the judge's ring procedure. If it is your first time in the ring, do not be over-anxious and run to the front of the line. It is much better to stand back and study how the exhibitor in front of you is performing. The judge asks each handler to 'stand' the dog, hopefully showing the dog off to his best advantage. The judge will observe the dog from a distance and from different angles, approach the dog, check his teeth, overall structure, alertness and muscle tone, as well as consider how well the dog 'conforms' to the standard. Most importantly, the judge will have the exhibitor move the dog around the ring in some pattern that he or she should specify (another advantage to not going first, but always listen since some judges change their directions, and the judge is always right!). Finally the judge will give the dog one last look before moving on to the next exhibitor.

If you are not in the top three at your first show, do not be discouraged. Be patient and consistent and you may eventually find yourself in the winning lineup. Remember that the winners were once in your

TIDINESS COUNTS

Surely you've spent hours grooming your dog to perfection for the show ring, but don't forget about yourself! Whilst the dog should be the centre of attention, it is

important that you also appear clean and tidy. Wear smart, appropriate clothes and comfortable shoes in a colour that contrasts with your dog's coat. Look and act like a professional.

shoes and have devoted many hours and much money to earn the placement. If you find that your dog is losing every time and never getting a nod, it may be time to consider a different dog sport or just enjoy your Bobtail as a pet.

WORKING TRIALS

Working trials can be entered by any well-trained dog of any breed, not just Gundogs or Working dogs. Many dogs that earn the Kennel Club Good Citizen Dog award choose to participate in a working trial. There are five stakes at both open and championship levels: Companion Dog (CD), Utility Dog (UD), Working Dog (WD), Tracking Dog (TD) and Patrol Dog (PD). As in conformation shows, dogs compete against a standard and if the dog reaches the qualifying mark, it obtains a certificate. Divided into groups, each exercise must be achieved 70 percent in order to qualify. If the dog achieves 80 percent in the open level, it receives a Certificate of Merit (COM); in the championship level, it receives a Qualifying Certificate. At the CD stake, dogs must participate in four groups: Control, Stay, Agility and Search (Retrieve and Nosework). At the next three levels, UD, WD and TD, there are only three groups: Control, Agility and Nosework.

Agility consists of three jumps: a vertical scale up a six-foot wall of planks; a clear jump over a basic three-foot hurdle with a removable top bar; and a long jump across angled planks stretching nine feet.

To earn the UD, WD and TD, dogs must track approximately one-half mile for articles laid from one-half hour to three hours previously. Tracks consist of turns and legs, and fresh ground is used for each participant.

PRACTISE AT HOME

If you have decided to show your dog, you must train him to gait around the ring by your side at the correct pace and pattern, and to tolerate being handled and

examined by the judge. Most breeds require complete dentition, all require a particular bite (scissor, level or undershot), and all males must have two apparently normal testicles fully descended into the scrotum. Enlist family and friends to hold mock trials in your garden to prepare your future champion!

SHOW QUALITY SHOWS

Whilst you may purchase a puppy in the hope of having a successful career in the show ring, it is impossible to tell, at eight to ten weeks, whether your dog will be a

contender. Some promising pups end up with minor to serious faults that prevent them from taking home a Best of Breed award, but this certainly does not mean they can't be the best of companions for you and your family. To find out if your potential show dog is show quality, enter him in a match to see how a judge evaluates him. You may also take him back to your breeder as he matures to see what he might advise.

The fifth stake, PD, involves teaching manwork, which is not recommended for every breed.

AGILITY TRIALS

Agility trials began in the United Kingdom in 1977 and have since spread around the world, especially to the United States, where they are very popular. The handler directs his dog over an obstacle course that includes jumps (such as those used in the working trials), as well as tyres, the dog walk, weave poles, pipe tunnels, collapsed tunnels, etc. The Kennel Club requires that dogs not be trained for agility until they are 12 months old. This dog sport proves to be great fun for dog and owner and interested owners should join a training club that has obstacles and experienced agility handlers who can introduce you and your dog to the 'ropes' (and tyres, tunnels, etc.).

FÉDÉRATION CYNOLOGIQUE INTERNATIONALE

Established in 1911, the Fédération Cynologique Internationale (FCI) represents the 'world kennel club.' This international body brings uniformity to the breeding, judging and showing of purebred dogs. Although the

Bobtails and their handlers participate in the ring during an outdoor show.

FCI originally included only four European nations: France, Holland, Austria and Belgium (which remains its headquarters), the organisation today embraces nations on six continents and recognises well over 300 breeds of purebred dog. There are three titles attainable through the FCI: the International Champion, which is the most prestigious; the International Beauty Champion, which is based on aptitude certificates in different countries; and the International Trial Champion, which is based on achievement in obedience trials in different countries. Dogs from around the globe participate in these impressive canine spectacles, the largest of which is the World Dog Show, hosted in a different country each year. FCI sponsors both national and international shows. The hosting country determines the judging system and breed standards are always based on the breed's country of origin.

The FCI is divided into ten 'Groups.' At the World Dog Show, the following Classes are offered for each breed: Puppy Class (6–9 months), Youth Class (9–18 months), Open Class (15 months or older) and Champion Class. A dog can be awarded a classification of Excellent, Very Good, Good, Sufficient and Not Sufficient. Puppies can be awarded classifications of Very Promising, Promising or Not Promising. Four placements are made in each class. After all sexes and classes are judged, a Best of Breed is selected. Other special groups and classes may also be shown. Each exhibitor showing a dog receives a written evaluation from the judge.

Besides the World Dog Show, you can exhibit your dog at speciality shows held by different breed clubs. Speciality shows may have their own regulations.

INDEX

*Page numbers in **boldface** indicate illustrations.*

Age 90
Agility trials 111, 153-154
Albinism 33
Allergy
—airborne 123
—food 124
American Kennel Club
—address 148
Ancylostoma caninum 136, **137**
Ascaris lumbricoides 136
Axelrod, Dr Herbert R 135
Backpacking 111
Bark 27
Bathing 71
Bearded Collie **10**, 17
Bedding 41
Boarding 81
Bobtail 31
Bones 43
Book of the Dog, The 9
Bowls 45
Breed name 14
Breed standard 26
Brown dog tick **134**
Brushing 70
de Buffon, Count 9
Burial 147
Canadian Kennel Club
—address 148
Canis lupus **13**
Cars 78
Cat 98
Caucasian 15
Caucasian Ovcharka **13**
Challenge Certificates 149-151
Champion 150
Champion Fairweather 11
Championship Shows 149
Chewing 92

Cheyletiella 135
China eye 28
Choke collar 45
Coat 32
—care 23
Collar 45, 98
Colostrum 62
Colour 32
Columella 9
Come 107
Commands 101
Cooper, Sidney 11
Coronavirus 121
Crate 39, 58, 78, 91, 94
—training 94
Creed, Pat 14
Crufts Dog Show 11, 149
Crying 58
Ctenocephalides **128,** 129
Ctenocephalides canis **126**
Dermacentor variabilis **133**
Destructive behaviour 145
Development schedule 90
Deworming programme 135
Diet 23
—adult 63
—puppy 62
—senior 65
Dirofilaria immitis **139**
Discipline 96
Distemper 121
Documentation 46
Dog Encyclopaedia 13
Dog flea **126**
Dog tick **133**
Double wall-eye 28
Down 103
Duke of Buccleuch 11
Dulux Paints 13
Dürer 9
Ear cleaning 75

Echinococcus multilocularis
138
Euthanasia 146
Exemption Shows 151
Exercise 67
External parasites 126-135
FCI 154
Fear aggression 101
Fear period 55
Fédération Cynologique
Internationale 154
—address 148
Feeding 60
Fence 49
Fernville, Lord Digby 14
First aid 125
Flea **126-131**
—life cycle of 127, **130**
Food
—allergy 124
—intolerance 124
—treats 110
Fosse, Mrs Fare 11
Freeman-Lloyd, Mr 11
Gainsborough 11
Glass, Mr and Mrs 14
Good Citizen Dog award 153
Grooming equipment 69
Handling 152
Harrison, Norman 13
Heartworm 138, **139**
Heel 108
Hepatitis 121
Herding instinct 20
Holistic medicine 140
Home preparation 38
Homeopathic remedies 141-142
Hookworm 136, **137**
—larva **137**
Hopwood, Aubrey 13
Hot spots 123
Housebreaking 88
—schedule 93

Identification 83

Illustrated Book of the Dog, The 13

Internal parasites 135-138

Italian Marrema Sheepdog 12

Johns, Rowland 13

Judge 152

Kennel Club, The 149

—address 148

—standard 27

Kennel cough 117, 121

Kennel Encyclopaedia 10

Komondor **10**, 16

Kuhn, Dwight R 131

Lead 44, 98

Leclerc, George Louis 9

Leptospirosis 121

Lice **134**

Life expectancy 144

Limited Shows 151

Lindane 135

Lord Nelson 14

Lupus 123

Mange 135

—mite **134**

Maremma Sheepdog 16

Matches 151

McCartney, Paul 18

Middle-Asian Ovcharka **11**, 15

Milk 63

Mis-marks 33

Mite 131, **134**, 135

—infestation 75, 135

Moist dermatitis 123

Mosshall Lady Joy 14

Movement 18, 32

Nail clipping 75

Neutering 118

Nipping 58

Obedience class 84, 110

Obesity 67, 145

OES Club of America 12

Old English Sheepdog Club 11

Open Shows 150

Our Friends, the Old English and Shetland Sheepdog 13

Ownership 35

Parasite

—bite 120

—external 126-135

—internal 135-138

Parvovirus 121

Pigment 28

Play 20

Polish Lowland Sheepdog **12**, 16

Polski Owczarek Nizinny **12**, 16

Pollen allergy 123

Psoroptes bovis **134**

Punishment 98

Puppy

—family introduction 50

—first night home 52

—health 117

—problems 54, 56

—training 86

Puppy-proofing 48

Rabies 121

Reinagle 9

Rhabditis **136**

Rhipicephalus sanguineus **134**

Roundworm 135, **136**

Russian Ovcharka 10, 15

Senior 144

Separation anxiety 58, 145

Sharpe, Mr and Mrs 13

Shaw, Vero 13

Shepton Daphnis Horsa 13

Shepton Mallet 12

Show Champion 149

Sit 101

Skin problems 119

—auto-immune 121

—hereditary 119

Smithfield Collie 10

Socialisation 54

South Russian Ovcharka **11**, 15

Sportsman's Cabinet, The 9

Standard 148

Stay 104

Stonehenge 9

Tail 17

—docking 10, 17

Tapeworm 135, **137**, 138

Thorndike's Theory of Learning 97

Thorndike, Dr Edward 97

Tick 131, **132-133**

Tickets 150

Tilley, H A 12-13

Tilley, W J S 12-13

Toxocara canis 135

Toys 42

Tracheobronchitis 117

Training 56

—equipment 98

Travelling 78

—air 79

—car 78

Treats 98

Tresaderm 135

Turner, Sidney 10

Twotrees Brandysnap 14

Uncinaria stenocephala 137

Undershot 30

Vaccinations 117

Van Eyck 9

Vesey-Fitzgerald, Brian 9

Veterinary surgeon 50, 113, 129, 135

Wall-eye 28

Water 65

Whining 58

White 33

Wolves 13

Working trials 153

World Dog Show 155

My Old English Sheepdog

PUT YOUR PUPPY'S FIRST PICTURE HERE

Dog's Name _____

Date _____ Photographer _____